Understanding Strategic Human Resource Management: A Playbook for Competitive Advantage

Salami Sule, FCIPM

Table of contents

Summary

Implementing strategic human resource management (SHRM) practices have the potential to make an organization stay on top and ahead of its competitors by using people as a competitive advantage. The objectives of this book are to critically appraise human resource (HR) philosophy and its applications, HR theories, the nature and characteristics of human resource management (HRM), and hard and soft HRM. The book also explains the strategies to achieve the goals of HRM, the core area of HRM, and how HRM function in a system and its diversity. The book appraises the concept, meaning, and nature of SHRM, HR metrics, competitive advantage, the concept of value chains, distinctive capabilities, and core competencies. The book also examines SHRM and the lessons it draws from strategic management, the elements, aims, and importance of HRM, strategic fit, strategic flexibility, and superior performance of an organization. The book explores human resource (HR) best practices, the best-fit approaches, and theoretical models of the best-fit approach and strategic choice. Case studies of the most capitalized companies in the world were used to draw key lessons on how they achieved success in their organization and business using SHRM practices.

When an organization or a company creates values for its customers, it ultimately becomes leverage for a competitive advantage against competitors. This can be achieved through gaining excellence and significant shares in the market niche selected. Management of organizations should critically examine and use best HRM practices and best-fit approaches as strategies in HR practices and applications to ensure competitive advantage and increase productivity and profitability. Contingent determination should not limit organizations in adopting HR best practices, but reality should prevail.

Introduction

Strategic human resource management (SHRM) has been defined as "a future-oriented process of developing and implementing human resource (HR) programs that address and solve business problems and directly contribute to major long-term business objectives" (1). Another definition of SHRM is "an approach to the development and implementation of HR strategies that are integrated with business strategies and enable the organization to achieve its goals (2)."

Implementing this HR strategy helps an organization to stay on top of its competitors using strategic human resource management (SHRM) as a competitive advantage (3).

It is important to state here that the need to align business strategies with HR to situate them in creating values for the organization and drive the achievement of its objectives led to the development of SHRM (4). A deep understanding of factors outside the organization and immediate business environment should determine these HR strategies, values, and their creation and should serve as great lessons for all managers (5). Strategic HRM is like a futuristic concept about the organization's business strategies aligning with the HR strategies with the purpose of integration that lead to seamless operations of the organization to achieve its competitive advantage and objectives. The HR strategies should drive and determine the vision, mission, and strategic plan to support the business strategies. This requires that there should be well-developed and fully implementable HR strategies supported by the organizational leadership and with HR functions and managers as part of the mainstream management team (2). Strategic HR is also about the HR functions that deal with developing and engaging employees by concentrating on the positive working experience of the individual to help the organization achieve its goals and objectives (6). The meeting points between HRM and strategic management concept defines the areas of SHRM and its focus. Therefore, in strategic management implementations and practices, these meeting points should be emphasized by an organization and HR managers (7). The goal of HRM in an organization should be how to make the employees happy, engaged, and motivated, and how to improve productivity and profitability.

Human Resource Philosophy

Human resource philosophy is the organization's leadership vision and attitude towards its human resource, which is informal and long-term to develop. The strategies employed by an organization to recruit, develop, educate, train, and manage its employees are determined by the components of the broader organization's policies, practices, and culture. These strategies are largely determined by the human resource philosophy of the organization.

The HR philosophy revolves around leadership and top management beliefs and assumptions about people and their work in an organization (8). It is about the organizational culture, beliefs, HR system, values, behaviors, and practices within an organization. This should be clearly articulated and written and determine the HR strategies, policies, and practices of an organization (2).

The Benefit of a Strong HR Philosophy

Organizational leadership and management that have the vision to develop its human resource as part of organization strategies will lead to more employee engagement and retention because of the satisfaction with the way their employer treats them as an employee. This satisfaction is derived from being valued and supported by their employer. This will lead to a trusted work environment that has developed between employees, managers, and the leadership of an organization and ultimately result in the development of a positive work culture. The need to set expectations and objectives as part of the overall goals of the organization as part of a clear HR policy should be derived from the HR strategies and philosophy. A trusted work environment in an organization with set expectations and objectives, and a clear HR policy will lead to increased performance by the employee and increased productivity by the organization. Employee loyalty can be fostered and promoted by the positive HR philosophy of an organization. Employees should be recognized and supported in the achievement of their work objectives and contribute to the overall organizational goals. The mechanism for this recognition should be embedded in the HR philosophy of an organization. This feeling of recognition and support can lead to employee retention and loyalty. Organizational competitive advantage strategies should include creating a culture that drives a positive work environment that can lead to employee engagement, retention, and loyalty and this should be driven by the HR philosophy of an organization that is envisioned by its leadership. A positive HR philosophy that is supported by the leadership and management of an organization can drive positive decision-making of the HR manager on employee development and how employees are managed. This by this means gives HR professionals and managers a strong hand to foster a positive work environment and culture. Using this playbook based on HR philosophy will give an organization a competitive advantage over its competitor and be productive and profitable.

The HR philosophy is all about valuing people's work for an organization and treating them with respect and dignity as the most important resource available to the organization. It is also about employee development in terms of the organization helping employees develop their skills and capabilities to be productive through training, education, and other means. The HR philosophy that promotes employee involvement by encouraging employees to take part in decision-making in an organization will encourage commitment and motivates an employee. The HR philosophy that pays a premium on the well-being of their employees in terms of their physical, social, and mental health will encourage a healthy and productive workforce. An organization should place a premium on the work-life balance of its employee and deliberately create this as part of HR policies.

In a competitive internal environment of a business enterprise or organization that drives innovation, an organization must tailor its HR policy to the recruitment of talents, which is immediately and regularly followed with training, an innovative workplace environment, motivation, and incentives to promote engagement, commitment, and increased productivity and profitability (9). This should be supported by the leadership and management of an organization.

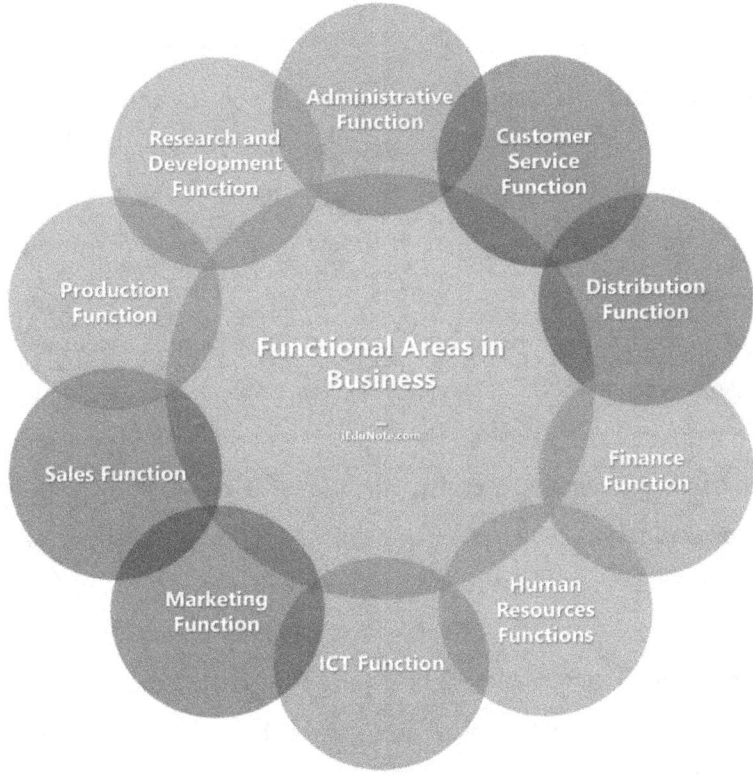

Figure 1: Functional analysis of business activities at Tesla by Michael Nelson (10)

Application of Human Resource Philosophy

Figure 1 displays the crossline of the different functions of business activities in an organization using Tesla as an example. It also illustrates the meeting point of human resource management and all the functional activities of the business at Tesla. It is important to see the interconnected of each of the functional aspects of the business and the functional area of the business as displayed in the large central circle in Figure 1. Human resource strategies should be designed to ensure all employees are aware of these various HR functions and how they are integrated to ensure improved and increased production of the business or organization's products or services. The leadership of the organization should promote and support this awareness through communication directly with each employee of that organization. Elon Musk, the CEO of Tesla promotes this direct communication from the leadership to all employees. He also advocated for an open flow of communication among employees. His HR philosophy has been quoted as "Anyone at Tesla can, and should, email/talk to anyone else according to what they think is the fastest way to solve a problem for the benefit of the whole company." He once wrote that "We are all in the same boat. Always view yourself as working for the good of the company and never your dept." This level of communication advocated by Elon Musk will give employees a sense of involvement in decision-making, true collaboration, and engagement of employees (11).

"Tesla Inc (Tesla) is an automotive and energy company. It designs, develops, manufactures, sells, and leases electric vehicles and energy generation and storage systems. The company produces and sells the

Model Y, Model 3, Model X, Model S, Cybertruck, Tesla Semi, and Tesla Roadster vehicles. Tesla also installs and maintains energy systems and sells solar electricity; and offers end-to-end clean energy products, including generation, storage, and consumption. It markets and sells vehicles to consumers through a network of company-owned stores and galleries. The company has manufacturing facilities in the US, Germany, and China and has operations across the Asia-Pacific and Europe. Tesla is headquartered in Austin, Texas, the US" (12).

Apple Inc. which produces the iPhone and MacBook computer, the leadership of company support and drives HR policies, processes, and practices approach that encourages retaining its creative workforce in adapting to the rapidly changing business environment in its industry and the intense competition among similar companies. These HR policies, processes, and practices put Apple Inc. in a position to constantly transform functional business activities to survive the competition and be ahead of its competitors. The leadership of Apple Inc. deliberately drives creativity and innovation among its employees through investing in human capital and the involvement of employees in decision-making (13).

"Apple Inc (Apple) designs, manufactures, and markets smartphones, tablets, personal computers (PCs), portable and wearable devices. The company also offers software and related services, accessories, and third-party digital content and applications. Apple's product portfolio includes iPhone, iPad, Mac, iPod, Apple Watch, and Apple TV. It offers various consumer and professional software applications such as iOS, macOS, iPadOS, watchOS, iCloud, AppleCare, Apple Pay, and accessories.

Apple sells and delivers digital content and applications through Apple Store, App Store, Apple Arcade, Apple News+, Apple Fitness+, Apple Card, Apple Pay, and Apple Music. The company has a business presence across the Americas, Europe, the Middle East, Africa, and Asia-Pacific. Apple is headquartered in Cupertino, California, the US" (14).

Apple Inc SHRM processes, techniques, and practices involve recruiting the talented and 'right candidates', by identifying potential employees that have been assessed to think out of the box and demonstrate some level of commitment to the company. Opportunities are deliberately created by Apple for its employees to develop a 'prospective' career and promote free thinking in design teams. Apple also encourages brainstorming for idea change. Major employees' contribution to Apple is recognized through rewards and designation as 'leaders' in a specifically designed and purposeful "Apple Fellows Program." This is to motivate and incentive employees who are star performers (15). Apple attracts talented employees by providing competitive remuneration packages, "flex benefits, periodical stock grants, and product discounts" for talented staff for their contribution to the company(16).

Human Resource Theories

1. **Commitment theory or organizational engagement**
    1.1. This is the theoretical explanation of individual and organizational characteristics that foster the commitment or engagement of an employee to an organization (17). This theory also explains the relationship between an organization

and the "employee's identification with, and involvement in, a particular organization" (18).

1.2. Mayer and Allen (1991) argue that there are three components of the commitment of employees in an organization which they argued to have emerged in most cases because of different precursor psychological behavior. The three components they described are:

1.2.1. "affective commitment", which is when an employee has an emotional attachment to the job in the workplace and the organization. It is a feeling of attachment, engagement, and loyalty to an organization.

1.2.2. "continuance commitment", is when an individual is concerned about the loss of finance or social resources, the individual will naturally belief there is an obligation to continue to stay with the organization. For example, if there are other benefits apart from the salary paid to the employee, this may drive the employee to continue to work for the organization especially if the employee perceives that these benefits e.g., health insurance, job security, availability for food, subsidized or free transportation to work, free or subsided accommodation, etc. cannot be secured easily in other organizations.

1.2.3. "normative commitment" is when social norms, patriotism, sense of loyalty sense of duty, or obligation make an employee stay with an organization e.g., employees who serve in the military and security services of a country (19) for an employee to be engaged and stay in an organization. Each of these three components has a different impact in terms of productivity of the commitment to the organization (20).

1.2.4. The fourth category of commitment is "calculative commitment," which is when the cost-benefit analysis is a major factor that the employee is considering whether to stay with the organization or leave. For example, when an employee considers the emolument and rewards received in an organization including severance packages such as gratuity and pension and weighs against losing part of this benefit if an employee leaves the organization.

1.3. Increased job satisfaction, retention of employees, positive attitude to work, and increased work performance and productivity has been associated with the commitment of employees to an organization. This Commitment can be achieved only if organizations provide support for their employees and create a positive work environment. This should be embedded in the HR policies and practices of the organization (21).

1.4. Other factors that can influence commitment to an organization are the employee's level of commitment, the qualities of the relationship between employees and their line managers or supervisor, and the relationship among employees themselves. Congruence between an employee's values and objectives with that of the organization's values and goals will also influence commitment.

1.5. The feelings an employee has towards an organization in the form of psychological attachments are important in determining the level of productivity the employee is willing to put into the job intuitively. This is important for an organization's success because it influences the level of engagement, retention of employees, and work attitude that potentially can promote the extraordinary performance of an employee.

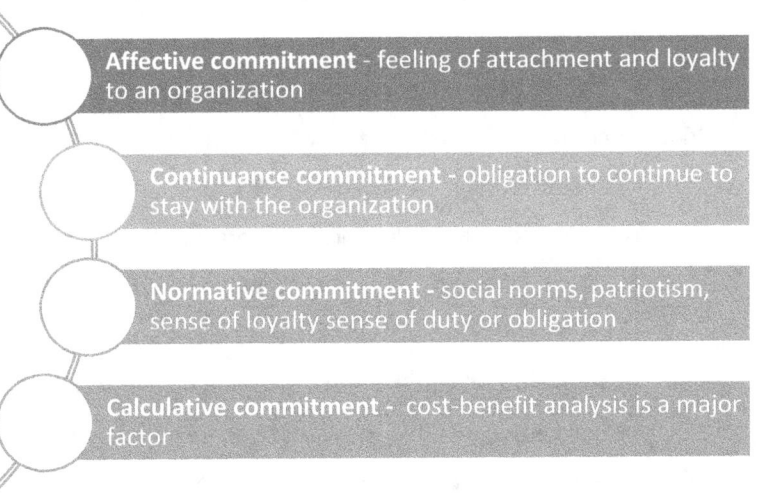

Figure 2: Commitment theories in human resource management

1. Organizational behavior theory

1.1. Organizational behavior theory describes the relationship between the functions of an organization, its structures, processes, and culture concerning the behavior of individuals in the organization (22).

1.2. The behavior of an individual or group of individuals within an organization is determined and impacted by individual, group, and organizational factors. The study of these effects and factors is to help managers have a better understanding and be able to forecast human behavior in an organization.

1.3. Several significant organizational theories have been developed over the years, starting with the most recent:

1.3.1. **Transformational Leadership Theory**: This theory recommends that leaders in organizations should encourage and motivate their employees as followers to reach their full potentials which can have a tremendous and transformative effect on organizational performance, productivity, and profitability. Transformational leadership has been found to help the employee develop intrinsic motivation through inspiration to achieve set and important goals. It has the potential to give employees self-confidence in assigned job schedules and responsibilities and to use assigned power to make decisions (23).

1.3.2. **Social Learning Theory**: This theory postulates that learning in an organization is driven by people observing and imitating the behavior of others. Employees' observation and adoption of the behavior of fellow employees, managers, and leaders in an organization can have a significant impact on organizational behavior and performance. This also includes modeling and emotional reaction to others (24). Bandura in 1977 extended the behaviorist theory of learning of conditioning and change in operant behavior as a result of the conditioning by adding the concept of observational learning and the mediating processes that is present in the environment (25). The mediating process involves individuals thinking through the behavior of a model before imitating it. This thinking process before adopting a behavior involves observation of the behavior, which is the stimulus, and imitation of the behavior or not, which is the response (26,27).

1.3.3. **Equity Theory**: This theory proposes that employees continuously assess whether they are being treated fairly by comparing their level of input, efforts, outcome, and output to other employees in the organization. This continuous assessment of equity and the consequent sense of inequity will ultimately lead the employee to adjust their behavior to reach a balance. subtle and variable factors affect an employee's perception of their relationship with their work and their employer. This theory is premised on the assumption that employees become less motivated to their job and committed to their organizations once they sense that their inputs and efforts are greater than the outcome and outputs they receive (28). The response of an employee to this inequity in the workplace may vary to the exhibition of de-motivation, disengagement, not committed, reduced effort, negative behavior, or, in extreme cases, perhaps even disruption or resignation. This passive resignation led to the development of the concept of 'quiet quitting' in HR, which refers to an employee only engaging in carrying out the minimum requirements of the assigned job schedule without extra time, effort, or interest necessary (29). However, the advancement of the theory will benefit from specificity regards over compensation of input and efforts in the area of areas of inequity determination, consequent dissatisfaction and response, and the variability in different contexts and environments (30,31).

1.3.4. **Theory X and Theory Y**: Douglas McGregor proposed this theory by suggesting that there are different assumptions held by managers about their employees' motivation and behavior. 'Theory X assumes that workers are inherently laid back and need to be controlled, while Theory Y assumes that workers are self-motivated and can be trusted to work towards organizational goals' (32).' Theory X has been criticized to have the potential to limit the full utilization of employees' potential and theory Y has been praised because it leads to higher motivation and a greater possibility of achieving individual employee and organizational goals. Although, there are few empirical studies on the effect of Theory X/Y behavior on the performance of employees. There is a need to demonstrate how, the effect and relationship of individual employees' Theory X/Y managerial attitudes and behaviors mediate job performance at both employees and team levels in different contexts, environments, and organizations (33).

1.3.5. **Hawthorne Effect**: This theory proposes that an employee's performance in an organization is influenced by social and psychological factors and is not limited to the workplace environment alone. This theory emerged from a series of studies carried out at the Hawthorne Works of the Western Electric Company. The Hawthorne effect occurs when an employee's behavior change as a result of the perception of being observed in an organization, rather than as a consequence of any intervention (34). When applying e Hawthorne effect theory to study employees' attitudes and behavioral changes in organizations, the psychological and social variables must be specified to determine the effect of the outcome under study (35). In summary, the Hawthorne effect is a change in behavior as a result of observation or assessment, which are examples of the psychology and social variables (36).

1.3.6. **Scientific Management The**ory: this Theory focuses on the systematic study of work processes to improve efficiency and productivity and was developed by Frederick Winslow Taylor in 1911. This theory proposes the analysis and synthesis of workflow to improve economic efficiency and labor productivity. The principles of scientific management as proposed by Taylor include 'science, not the rule of thumb;' 'harmony, not discord;' 'mental revolution;' 'cooperation, not individualism;' 'development of every person to his greatest efficiency.' Its contemporary application to workplace management includes job analysis, synthesis, logic, work ethics, standardization of best practices, scaling up of production, organizational learning, and transfer of knowledge (37). The application of the principles of scientific management to employees and organizations in a simple or complex situation has the potential to yield outstanding results (38).

1.3.7. **Maslow's hierarchy of needs** (39) – this theory stipulates that individuals have needs that are hierarchical to be motivated at different stages of attainment or fulfillment in life. These needs are:

1.3.7.1. Physiological needs – fundamental needs necessary for the survival of an individual, for example, the need for food, water, shelter, rest, etc. If physiological needs are not met, an individual will not be able to function effectively and can become sick and die.

1.3.7.2. Safety needs – a sense of security and protection from physical and psychological harm at normal periods and at times of turbulence, crises, stress, or dangerous situation when there may be a threat to the sense of well-being. Examples are a safe house, job and income security, access to healthcare, and protection from the elements in the environment including protection from physical harm.

1.3.7.3. Social needs – for human interaction and feeling of belonging, love, and companionship to safeguard emotional and mental health. For example, starting and nurturing relationships with friends, intimate relationships, or with family members, and engagement in social, community, and professional groups.

1.3.7.4. Esteem needs – a sense of self-worth and respect for others. There are two categories:

1.3.7.4.1. Self-esteem – the feeling of self-worth and self-respect. The feeling of competency and worthy of respect

1.3.7.4.2. External esteem – the respect and admiration we receive from others. Examples are status, recognition, and appreciation from others.

1.3.7.4.3. If esteem needs are not met, there may be feeling of inferiority, unvalued and unmotivated.

1.3.7.5. Self-actualization needs – is the zenith of psychological development by fulfilling an individual potential and best version of self, achieving sense of purpose and meaning in life. For example, personal growth and development, creativity and sense of self-awareness, deeper understanding of self and an individual place in the world seeing things from multiple perspectives, thinking independently, and making a decision based on an individual value and belief. Without the lower level of psychological needs being met, an individual will not be able to focus on fulfilling their potential and achieving self-actualization.

1.3.8. **Expectancy Theory**: This theory explains the mental processes regarding how an individual makes decisions to choose a course of action or not, the mental process, and the act of choosing. Intrinsically an individual makes choices rationally choosing behaviors they consider or believe will give them the most benefit and favorable outcome. This theory explains what value an individual place on motivation, and depend on the understanding of good performance, having the capacity to deliver it, and necessarily the value of the rewards as a result of the high performance (40,41). This Theory was developed by

Victor Vroom of the Yale School of Management, who explained the importance to link rewards to a performance by an organization. The Theory also emphasizes that employees in an organization must want or desire the reward and merit it (42). The theory has three components, namely 'expectancy,' 'instrumentality,' and, 'valence.' Expectancy is an individual believes that their effort will lead to a desirable performance, which will motivate individuals to put in their best effort. Instrumentality is an individual belief linking high performance with certain outcomes and rewards such as promotion. Valence is the value an individual place on outcome or rewards that is a consequence of high performance. The motivation for an individual in this theory depends on the value placed on the outcome or rewards. The motivation for an individual in this theory depends on the value placed on the outcome or rewards. Contrasting models of expectancy theory have been developed by industrial and organizational psychology. Among the most important contrasting model is the question of rationality on the part of the individual in making a choice behavior which might be ignored and ambiguous in some of the components of expectancy Theory (43).

2. **Motivation theory**

2.1. Individuals are driven to put in their best to an organization to achieve defined goals or results. The motivational theory explains this phenomenon that affects goal-directed behavior in an employee. This motivation can be from the individual or intrinsic motivation that has been described to be associated with factors in the workplace that drives an employee due to outcome success. The external motivation which has been termed Expectancy theory is external to the employee and characterized by rewards either financial or non-financial (44).

2.2. There are various associated theories to Motivation theory which include i. Maslow's hierarchy of needs, ii. Hertzberg's two-factor theory, iii. McClelland's theory of needs, iv. Vroom's theory of expectancy, and v. McGregor's theory X and theory Y. Motivation is a psychological state that can fluidity depending on the work environment and how leaders create a conducive and well-motivated work environment for increased productivity and employee engagement (45).

3. AMO (ability, motivation, opportunity) theory

3.1. The AMO theory was developed to explain the relationship between human resource management and the performance of employees (46–48). The AMO acronym stands for ability, motivation, and opportunity, which has been explained to strongly influence performance (49). The AMO context was initially developed by Baily (50) and further developed by Appelbaum (47). The framework is designed with the assumption that an employee performs well when he or she has inherent capacity or capability, and this performance is augmented by a conducive working environment that creates the opportunity to perform and the need for motivation for the employee to achieve high performance.

3.2. Appelbaum et al developed the model required for high-performance work systems (HPWS) (47) and argued that organizations are more likely to achieve their goals when employees are given the necessary information, engaged and empowered by their managers, and made to take increased responsibilities and make guide decision about work activities.

3.3. A high-performance work system has been described as a mix of HRM practices to promote employee and organizational performance, which must be well-coordinated and aligned with HR practice to the organization's strategies and goals (50,51).

4. Human capital theory

4.1. The knowledge and skills of employees are the capital that can help an organization gain that desirable competitive advantage and achieve its goals faster (52). This capital termed human capital is an intangible asset that most organizations may not appreciate as a key factor of production. The value created by an employee to the organization has been explained in human capital theory. Training and education of employees have been explained as the best way to develop human capital and add value to the individual and organization (53,54).

5. **Resourced-based theory**

   5.1. The resource-based theory explains the value of resources that are scarce and very difficult to replicate or acquire. If an organization own or acquire such resources including human resource, it will give it a competitive advantage (55). This has been explained to be responsible for efficient, effective, and better performance by an organization (56).

6. **Contingency theory**

   6.1. Contingency theory explained that "no size fits all" strategy or means of organizing or managing resources or leading in an organization. That some organizational management or leadership styles that fit one situation may not fit another situation (57). The effective and efficient management of an organization or leadership style is dependent on both internal and external factors that may act as constraints. These constraints or contingency factors may include the characteristics of the organization, its structure, its operational setup, the economic, social, political, and geographical environment, the technology available, and the level of infrastructure development (58). In summary, there is no one best practice to manage an organization whether simple or complex and the most effective approach to managing an organization may depend on the context, environment, current situation, the individual employees, and the type of organization (59).

The Nature of Human Resource Management

Human resource management (HRM) has been defined as the management of the human component of work-related resources as related to employment within an organization (60). It has also been defined as " …. primarily concerned with the management of people within organizations, focusing on policies and systems (61)." When strategically managed, HR also involves the efficient and effective use of individuals in an organization to help gain a competitive advantage and achieve organizational goals and objectives.

Traditionally, HR involves the process of managing the workforce in an organization. The nature of HR includes recruitment, selection, training, development, compensation, benefits, and performance management. This is multifaceted and HR involves a variety of activities in the workplace that aim to maximize the potential of employees and align their performance with the organization's goals.

The HRM as a distinctive discipline and approach to people's management in the workplace is to achieve competitive advantage by strategically utilizing highly engaged and committed employees through the integration of HR theories, principles, practices culture, structure, and management techniques (62).

The HRM covers activities such as human capital management, knowledge management, organization design and development, resourcing (workforce planning, recruitment and selection, and talent management), employee relations, and employee well-being.

Beer et al in 1984 stressed the need to look at HR with a futuristic perspective in managing individuals and see individuals in an organization as an asset rather than as a liability. They also coined the two characteristic features of HR (63):

"1.   line managers or supervisors or team leaders accept more responsibility for ensuring the alignment of competitive strategy and HR policies.

2.   HR mission of setting policies that guide how HR activities are developed and implemented in ways that make them more mutually reinforcing."

Fombrum et al in 1984 in their explanation of the "matching model" identified the importance of aligning HR and organizational systems to ensure congruence between HR and organization strategies (64). This led to the statement that: "The critical management task is to align the formal structure and human resource systems so that they drive the strategic objectives of the organization (2,64)." This gave birth to the concept of strategic human resource management and based on their work and other similar academics in the US lead to the   transformation of the old term 'personnel management' to 'human resources management (65).'

The following theme of HRM was identified by Legge (65):

1.   To reinforce an appropriate organizational culture or to change it requires integration of business strategies at the planning stage with human resources policies

2.   One source of competitive advantage in an organization is human resources and therefore should be treated as a valuable resource

3. Creating an environment and culture that foster willingness in an individual in the workplace to act flexibly "act flexibly in the interests of the adaptive organization's pursuit of excellence."
4. To promote commitment in an individual in a workplace, there should be consistent HR policies that are mutually agreeable between employees and employers

The assumption is that HR decisions are an important strategy for organizational development, to achieve its goals and competitive edge with its employees (3). The human resource manager's role is to plan the workforce to achieve the organization's goals. They work with top management to ensure that there is the right mix of workforce with the requisite knowledge base and skills to achieve these goals. They develop and implement HR strategies and align HR strategies to the business strategies of the organization through the initiative and development of HR policies and practice guidelines. The HR manager in an organization is expected to bridge the gap between employees and management relationships by addressing expectations, demands, grievances, etc.

Characteristics of Human Resource Management (HRM)

The simplistic explanation of the characteristics of human resource management is that HRM is about people's management in a workplace environment by talent hunt, selecting, training, assessing, and rewarding the workforce. The characteristics of HRM extend to leadership and culture in the workplace, communication, dynamism through flexibility, team spirit, and giving work its appropriate names.

In theory, HRM characteristics are as stated by Armstrong (2):

"Strategic with an emphasis on integration; Commitment-orientated; Based on the belief that people should be treated as assets (human capital); Unitarist rather than pluralist, i.e. based on the belief that management and employees share the same concerns and it is therefore in both their interests to work together, rather than the belief that the interests of employees will not necessarily coincide with their employers; Individualistic rather than collective in its approach to employee relations; A management-driven activity – the delivery of HRM is a line management responsibility; and focused on business, moral and social values

Hard and Soft HRM

Hard and soft HRM depict the diversity of the assumptions and theory of HRM (3), which are two different approaches to HRM. This diversity can be illustrated by the *'human'* and *'resource'* components of HRM. The human aspect helps to explain soft HRM, and the resource aspect help to explain hard HRM (66,67). The Hard HRM sees HR as one of the economic factors or as other resources to be planned, quantified, measured, and analyzed as a business strategy for efficiency d productivity. While in contrast, soft HRM, also known as humanistic or developmental HR emphasizes employees as 'valued assets' to be nurtured and developed; and as a source of 'competitive advantage' (61). Soft HRM is about human relationships, interaction, communication, motivation, and an individualistic perspective in the management of HR (68). Soft HR has been likened to McGregor's theory Y and hard HRM to McGregor's theory X (69). The desire in theory is for there to be soft HRM, but in reality always throws up hard HRM because of the external environmental factors, particularly the economic factors that force the organization to put its survival above that of an individual (70). Therefore, reality forces the existence of both soft and hard HRM in an organization that often develops the appropriate mixture of both soft and hard HRM in the management of HR to fit into the organizational business and HR strategies and culture.

Harm HR is also known as traditional or strategic HRM and involves a more formal and structural approach to HRM that places a premium on processes and procedures to control the business or mandate of the organization. This HRM approach is all about achieving organizational goals. Soft HR is the flexible and informal aspect of HR that may not be structural in its approach. It emphasizes the development, engagement, and empowerment of the employees, and this approach is all about motivating employees to be productive. It is important to appreciate and understand these hard and soft HR approaches to HR practice in the context of culture, goals, values, and type of organization. The use of a combination of these two approaches may complement each other, and the right mix can be a fulcrum in the leverage for competitive advantage for an organization (71).

The Goals of HRM

The main goals of HRM are to drive and improve organizational effectiveness, promote a positive work environment, a happy workplace for the employees, and increase productivity. Establishing workplace culture plays a critical role in achieving HR goals. The organization's culture when establish should foster employee motivation and job satisfaction. The objectives of HRM are to create a highly skilled workforce to ensure employees are motivated to contribute meaningfully to the organizational goals through a focus on developing an organizational culture that encourages this.

The highlighted goals of HRM are:

1. Helps the organization reach its goals.
2. Ensures effective utilization, engagement, and maximum development of HR.
3. Identifies and satisfies the needs of individuals.
4. Achieves and maintains high morale among employees.
5. Provides the organization with well-trained and well-motivated employees.
6. Enhances employee capabilities to perform the present job.
7. Inculcates a sense of team spirit, teamwork, and inter-team collaboration.

Strategies to Achieve the Goals of HRM

The traditional strategies for achieve HR goals are

1. human resource or manpower planning,

2. Recruitment, selection, and placement of personnel,

3. training and development of employees,

4. appraisal of the performance of employees,

5. remuneration of employees,

6. setting general and specific management policies for the organization, and

7. developing and maintaining motivation for workers through incentives.

Contemporary HR practice has shown different effective strategies to achieve HR goals in a competitive world. These are some of the strategies used by an organization to achieve the goal of HRM and manage its workforce.

1. **Set clear and specific goals and develop an HR plan**: This is the first step in achieving strategies for HR goals and also the first step HR plan. The set HR goals must align with the organizational goals and objectives to garner and focus all efforts of employees and management to achieve HR goals. Once the goals are set, it is imperative to develop HR plans by carefully developing a step-by-step action plan to include objectives for each goal, specific activities, targets, timelines, resources required, and responsible team members assigned. It is important that as part of this HR plan, communication channels are included in achieving HR goals. Open and clear communication channels within the organization, particularly between HR and other departments are identified and included in the HR plan.

2. **Recruitment and selection**: Employing the right talent for the right work position is one of the most important aspects of HRM practice. The organizational goals and objectives should align with the recruitment and selection strategy. The focus is

to attract and engage the most qualified talent with the required knowledge, skill, attitude, and experience.

3. **Training and development**: The investment of an organization in the training and development of its workforce is to assist them to develop and acquire new knowledge, and skills to improve their performance and be more effective in their work position and job schedule. This strategy is to enable employees to continue to contribute to organizational goals through training and talent development. This should be aligned and tailored to meet the training needs of employees.

4. **Performance Management**: This involves setting performance goals with employee engagement, assessing performance, and rewarding good performance. It also involves feedback and coaching, which can assist employees to improve their performance and contribute more effectively to organizational goals. Performance management should use measurable and objective criteria that should desirably be in congruence with the organizational goals.

5. **Employee Engagement**: The engagement of employees in an organization is aimed at acquainting them with the organizational goals and objectives to encourage and increase their commitment and productivity. It can also be used to motivate employees. The engagement of employees that also focus on recognition and rewarding performance can lead to the creation of a positive work environment and opportunities for the employees and the organization's growth and development. There is a need for an organization to develop

and implement policies for the engagement of employees and design a workplace environment for employees with opportunities for growth, development, and rewarding performance. Employee engagement, if properly implemented will lead to increase productivity in an organization.

6. **Diversity and Inclusiveness**: Organization leadership that promotes diversity and inclusiveness in the workplace environment has the potential to attract talents, increase innovation and creativity; and foster a culture of respect and inclusiveness. The focus on diversity and inclusion should be tailored to provide equal opportunities for all the workforce in an organization, to use it to improve productivity.

7. **Succession Planning**: the continuity and stability of an organization can be best safeguarded by deliberate succession planning by the leadership of an organization. This will minimize the turnover of top and strategic employees. This involves identifying high-performance and committed employees that can be trained and developed to take up management and leadership positions in an organization which

is   good   for   leadership   transitions.

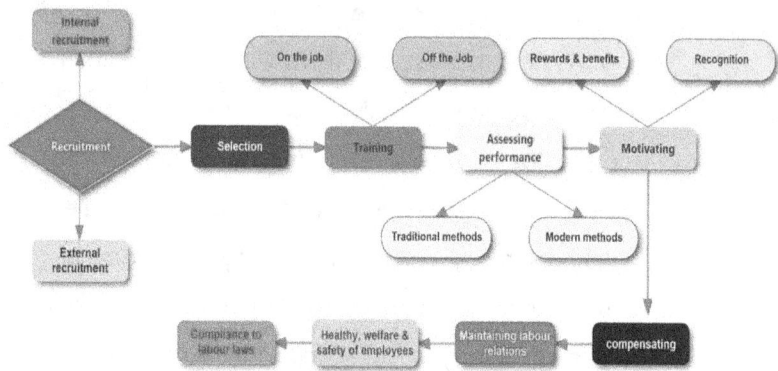

Figure 3: HRM Processes and Characteristics – courtesy of Whatishumanresourcemanagement (72).

The Core Areas of HRM

1. **Strategic Human Resource Management (SHRM)**: Strategic human resources management (SHRM) is simple a process of aligning organizational goals and HR goals and practices. This involves the integration of HR strategy and practices with the overall organizational strategy. This is to ensure that the organization has the right complement and mix of highly skilled workforce to achieve organizational strategic goals. The key components of SHRM are i. the core competencies and capabilities to achieve organizational goals are identified and developed; ii. design and develop HR policies and practice that align with organizational strategies, goals, culture, and values; iii. attracting and retaining highly

knowledgeable and skilled workforce through the design and development of HR programs targeted at motivating the best talent; iv. designing and developing policies and programs that align organization strategic goals and objectives with HR metrics and performance measures; and v. the Continuous monitoring and evaluation of organizational HR policy implementation, practices, and programs to ensure they are meeting organizational strategic goals.

2. **Resourcing and Talent Planning**: This is the aspect of HRM that is concerned with attracting, recruiting, and retention of highly skilled and capable employees to meet the current and future needs of an organization. It starts with the identification of human resource needs by assessing the knowledge, skill, and experience of the existing workforce. The organization's HR manager in conjunction with the organizational management then develops and implements strategies to fill the gap and meet this workforce's needs. Resourcing and talent planning ultimate objectives are to safeguard that the right employee is attracted and employed and put in the right position at the right time to achieve the goals and objectives of the organization.

Resourcing and talent planning approaches include:

2.1. Talent acquisition by filling current and future talent gaps and needs from outside the organization with new talents.

2.2. Succession for employees to function in future roles involves developing opportunities and preparing them in the form of deliberate succession planning by an organization. This involves filling critical roles in the organization including leadership positions.

2.3. Career development involves giving employees the opportunity for growth and development in their careers by providing training and training opportunities, job rotation, supervision, and mentoring.

2.4. Performance management entails the processes of setting performance expectations, assessing performance, providing feedback, coaching, and mentoring employees to improve their performance and achieve their career goals.

3. **Integrated Performance Management System**: This is a process whose objective is to establish processes to assist employees contribute meaningfully to the organization's success and goals. Integrated performance management system (IPMS) should be designed to:

3.1. ensure that the performance of employees is aligned with the organizational goals and objectives.

3.2. engagement of the employee by assigning meaningful and fulfilling job schedules and duties.

3.3. flexibility to adapt and change job roles when there is a new development or shift in the organization's goals and objectives in response to changing internal and external environments.

3.4. facilitation by the HR managers and organizational management of HR strategies, reviewing operations environment and processes, and managing workforce data on employee's performance for decision making.

Although IPMS implementation in an organization has the potential to lead to unhealthy internal rivalry and competition among employees for job status, position, and benefits. The IPMS benefits the organization through improved efficiency and effectiveness, reduced cost, customer satisfaction, and improvement in operations. The IPMS requires commitment from the leadership of the organization because it requires a lot of resources, and on the part of the managers and employees, a lot of patience to realize IPMS benefits. The IPMS requires preparation, a communication plan, gaining employees and manager acceptance, a training program on the acquisition of required skills, performing a pilot test, ongoing monitoring and evaluation, and a lot of administrative time.

4. **Total Rewards and Remuneration Management**: Total reward is the aggregate compensation or remuneration that an employer gives to an employee. It is also referred to as the sum of financial and non-financial benefits that an employee receives. This consists of remuneration in terms of salary or wages, plus other benefits, incentives, and other forms of compensation. Often organizations have incentives and welfare packages for their employees such as paid leave, health insurance of whole health care service or even hospital within the organization, transportation services, provision of subsidized or free food, contributory pension scheme, flexibility in working schedule, training, and development. Total rewards also include recognition, employee career development, a functional working environment with available working tools, and a positive

working environment. A total reward that includes some or all of the mentioned incentives is designed by the organization to encourage employees' improved performance and productivity. It also helps in attracting and retaining highly skilled and the best talent in the industry.

A remuneration package is a specific financial compensation given by an employer to an employer for specific work done. This usually consists of a basic salary and allowance, some organizations may pay bonuses, commissions, or another financial reward based on performance or a specific role or assignment. The difference between a remuneration package and a total reward is that a remuneration package only involves monetary compensation given to an employee.

Some factors can determine the total reward paid to an employee by an organization or employer. These factors may include i. position in the organization, job role, talent, performance, experience, and the wage structure of the organization. The engagement and motivation of workers are part of the aim and focus of implementing both financial and non-financial reward packages for employees.

5. **Employee Learning and Talent Development**: This includes learning and training activities that enhance employees' learning, improving, or acquiring new knowledge, attitude, or skills. There is an informal and formal way of employee learning and development. The formal process includes a formal training program, workshops, or conferences designed to ensure the learning and talent

development of employees to improve performance. Informal methods of learning and talent development are the process of learning on the job while performing a task and carrying out the job schedule, it also includes mentoring and coaching activities. All activities in the workplace that support employee learning and growth are talent development. Talent development which should aim at reducing the skill gap is a process and a program that should be designed and implemented to meet organizational needs and goals and to individual professional or career growth and development. Different learning approaches should be used tailored to different learning styles of employees with incorporated regular assessment to evaluate the effectiveness of the training and talent development programs.

Learning and development (L&D) encompass talent development, training, learning, and performance improvement. The ultimate objective of L&D is to improve productivity towards achieving organizational goals and career growth of employees by enhancing knowledge and skill acquisition. For an organization to be competitive and successful in the long term, there is a need to invest continuously in employees learning and development to continually develop the knowledge, attitude, and skills of its employees.

6. **Organizational Development and Change Management**: This involves planned interventions that focus on improving systems, processes, and culture. Organizational development is a systematic process to improve organizational effectiveness, efficiency, and employee welfare. Change management is managerial and

individual activities to support transitioning of individuals, teams, and organizations from the current state to desired future state. The two concepts of organizational development and change management are related but different in focus and scope. Organizational development focuses on enhancing organizational effectiveness, and efficiency through changes in the structure, processes, systems, and culture within an organization. Change management focuses on managing the workforce in the period of change, which include preparation, understanding, the needs, and support for the change. Organizational development (OD) and change management (CM) are essential functions of the organization to help adapt to changing and highly competitive operating environment to help meet organizational goals. The processes and structures for OD and CM include i. employees training and leadership development programs, ii. diversity, inclusion initiatives, and change management program, iii. talent management and performance management system, iv. employee's engagement and succession planning program, and v. process improvement and team building activities. The OD and CM activities are planning, communication, training, coaching, and evaluation.

Organizational development follows the development process cycle which includes i. problem identification, ii. situational assessment, iii. action planning, iv. implementation plan, iv. Data gathering, v. analysis of data and results, vi. feedback and vii. repeat the cycle.

ORGANIZATION DEVELOPMENT STRATEGY:
Five Phases to Designing and Implementing

ENTRY
Exploring the problem, opportunities, or situation. Output is an engagement contract or project plan with expectations and agreement on scope.

DIAGNOSIS
The fact-finding phase. A data collection process where information is gathered, analyzed, and reviewed.

FEEDBACK
Exploring information for understanding, clarity, and accuracy. Output is an action plan that outlines the change solutions to be developed, and defined success indicators based on the information and data analysis.

SOLUTION
Correcting the problem, closing gaps, improving, or enhancing performance, or seizing opportunities. Output is a plan or suggested training course curriculum.

EVALUATION
Collecting data to determine if the initiative is meeting goals and achieving defined success indicators. Output is an evaluation report with recommendations for continuous improvement.

Figure 4: Phases of Organizational development strategies – courtesy Association of Talent Development (ATD) 'What is organizational development' (73).

The process in the design and implementing organizational development strategies is structured into five phases:

1. The entry phase involves presentation, exploration, and identifying the problem, opportunities, or situation.

2. The diagnosis or assessment phase involves the collection of data and engagement of all stakeholders in the organization with the relevant information gathered about the presenting problem that was analyzed.

3. The feedback phase involves giving back to the organization of analyzed information; exploration of the information for

understanding, clarity, and accuracy; review of preliminary agreements about scope and resource requirements; and the beginning of ownership of data by the organization. Development of an action plan listing the solutions to be developed to ensure change takes place, success indicator definition-based analysis of data, and review of information.

4.   The design, development, and implementation of the solution phase involve determining measures to solve the problem and improve organizational effectiveness, efficiency, and performance. The output may be the "development of a communication plan, a role-and-responsibility matrix, a training plan, a training curriculum, an implementation plan, a risk management plan, an evaluation plan, or a change management plan" (73).

5.   The evaluation phase involves continuous monitoring and evaluation to determine if the identified solution is meeting the identified succus indicators and goals. The evaluation report is generated for meeting continuous improvement in the organization.

The OD involves a collaborative and systematic approach to change management which might require the involvement of OD practitioners as external consultants or specialists.

The benefits of OD include improved productivity, communication and collaboration, job satisfaction, and employee engagement. It also increases innovation and the provision of improved service delivery to customers or the public. It also helps organizations to adapt to changing environmental factors affecting operations, and external challenges and to stay competitive.

The change management (CM) process is a structural and collaborative activity that involves all stakeholders. There are several key stages in change management.

The preparation stage involves the identification of the need for change and a change management plan is developed by setting objectives and assessing the potential impact of the proposed change. Identify stakeholders and develop a communication strategy.

The implementation stage involves putting the change activities into action. This is done by training employees, enhancing communication activities with stakeholders concerning the expectations of the change activities and potential problems, and continuous monitoring and evaluation of the change process. It is important to constitute and manage a change team in the organization to see through the change process successfully.

Post-implementation of the change stage involves evaluation of the success of the change by identifying the effectiveness of the change and areas of improvement. This is when the result of the implementation of change is communicated to all stakeholders in the organization and the celebration of success and learning from failure in the implementation of the change.

The benefit of effective change management includes improved productivity, increased employee engagement, enhanced customer satisfaction, and a more adaptable, nimble agile, and responsive organization.

7. **Industrial and Employee Relations**: This is the interrelationship between employer and employee, labor or trade union, employers organization, and the government (74). The broader term currently in use is 'Employment relations.' This relationship is complex but important for establishing a healthy relationship between employees and the management of an organization to the main harmony in the workplace.

The need for good employment relations is to promote increased organizational effectiveness, efficiency, improved performance, and productivity. It can lead to engagement and low employee turnover or a high retention rate arising for work satisfaction. Good employment relations can also lead to fewer conflicts and reduced stress in the workplace for both employees and managers in an organization. Employees who are motivated, engaged, and happy in the workplace tend to positively influence their colleagues can lead to commitment and loyalty to the organization, less absenteeism, and a feeling of being part of the organization (75). Indeed Editorial Team (76), the acclaimed number 1 job site in the world proposes some tips to improve employment relations like requesting employee's feedback in an open dialogue; employee to be acquainted with the organizational mission and vision; employees feel valued; work-life balance promotion by the employer; and create opportunity for career advancement and development.

Employment relations offer the opportunity for employer and employee to have a good relationship that benefits the organization and the employees. These benefits include ensuring and promoting continuous production of goods and services without interruption and reducing conflict, disputes, or unrest from employment-related issues that can lead to a strike and other industrial actions and tension between the organization, employees, and trade union. Good employment relationship fosters the effectiveness of an organization to be efficient through the good utilization of resources, motivates employees, and promotes peace in the workplace. Well-established employment relations in an organization promote feedback dialogue leading to social dialogue and social interaction between employees and their managers and among employees. Good Employment relations can lead to better remuneration, rewards in the workplace, and good working relations and social justice (77).

8. **Employee Engagement**: This denotes the degree and level of dedication, commitment, involvement, and enthusiasm that an employee has toward their work schedule, organization, and goals. The feeling of passion and wiliness to go beyond and above what an employee's work schedule entails and contribute to the success of their organization determine if an employee is engaged or not. Engagement is associated with and is influenced by higher job satisfaction, productivity, and retention rate. A positive work environment, effective communication, opportunities for career growth and development, and rewarding employee contribution are some of the drivers of employee engagement. Measuring employee

engagement through surveys, observation focus group discussions, or individual or group interviews can give managers and organizations clues about the level of employee engagement. This knowledge can guide the organization to identify an area that needs improvement to enhance employee engagement to improve organizational effectiveness and performance. The strength of the emotional and mental connection that an employee connects to the work, their co-employees, managers, and organization essentially define what is employee engagement. This is usually exhibited by the level of enthusiasm and dedication an employee feels toward their work. Examples of employee engagement include i. how the leadership of the organization connects or bonds with employees; ii. Working teams and creating team spirit; iii. Employees buying into and imbibing organization values and culture, iv. Rewarding effort and recognition of performance by the leadership of the organization,

and v. involvement of employees in **Box 1: Tesla HR Practice summary** (78,79).

planning and formulating strategies for the organization.

To measure employee engagement, the organization should identify and determine the outcome of engagement to measure through studies of employees. This can be done by studies combining survey methods, focus group discussions (FGD), and individual or group interviews of representatives of all sectors or departments in the organization. This is to have holistic data on what is important to the employees. Then perform a driver analysis from the result of these studies. Driver analysis also known as relative importance analysis estimates the importance of a series of predictor variables in predicting an outcome of interest or variable. That is, driver analysis is the statistical method for assessing the relationship between different variables (80). Driver analysis helps the organization to understand the driver behind employee engagement and the measure of employees' engagement metric. The only way an organization can drive employee engagement and growth is by first understanding what matters to your employees and then focusing on them (81). The added benefit of understanding employee engagement and focusing on them will lead to lower employee turnover, increased customer experience, improved employee initiative and ability to act with little supervision, higher job satisfaction, good relations, better level of safety, and increased productivity and performance (82).

9. **Diversity and Inclusiveness**: These two ideas drive workplace values and culture. Diversity includes and relates to any characteristics of individuals or groups that make them different from each other. Inclusion can be described as deliberate actions, integration strategies, or establishing cultural and social values to accept and embraces those with different background or characteristics (83). Diversity has been referred to as the 'what and inclusiveness as the 'how.' Organization embracing diversity should create a safe environment that nurtures and celebrate the understanding of the differences in individuals and groups. The complete range of human expression and experience in an organization should be seen as diverse. This diverse range includes; place of birth, tribe or ethnicity, nationality, religion, level of education or background, socio-

"According to Forbes, Google is building a culture where employees feel valued with a sense of psychological safety and empowerment."

- "**Google** has contracted Performance Paradigm to develop their own diversity, equity, and inclusion programs.
- Through shared experiences and community building, the is a disruptive way to truly incorporate DEI within **Google**."
- Google is shifting the conversation around diversity, equity, and inclusion (DEI) to create more deeply engaged leaders and teams.

economic status, gender, sexual orientation, disability, culture, and personality.

The essence of inclusion in an organization is to recognize an individual worth irrespective of how different they are from each other. This requires a mindset shift and change in organizational culture. The ultimate objective of diversity and inclusiveness in the workplace is to promote a sense of belonging and the added benefit of creating a culture that makes employees to be engaged as a result of this sense of belonging.

The effect of diversity and inclusiveness in an organization:

Box 2: Google Diversity, Equity, and Inclusion (DEI) Practice (84).

1. The mix of knowledge, attitude, skills, and experience that a diverse workforce brings to an organization can drive

innovation and creativity which lead to long-term productivity, growth, and competitive advantage.

2. Creating a safe workplace environment that gives an employee a sense of belonging can lead to a more emotional and mental investment of the employees in the job and organization and therefore more employee engagement with co-employees, managers, and the organization. This will encourage collaboration and increased productivity.

3. Diverse and inclusive workplace culture helps create a healthy, productive, and cooperative work environment that may lead to reduced stress, conflicts, and good health and well-being of employees. Diversity and inclusiveness ultimately lead to a sense of more trust, belonging, engagement, and commitment by the employees (85).

How HRM functions as a system and its diversity

The Academy to Innovate HR identified twelve key functions of HR, which are: 1. Human resource planning, 2. Recruitment and selection, 3.Performance management, 4. Learning and development, 5. Career planning, 6. Function evaluation, 7. Rewards, 8. Industrial relation, 9. Employee participation and communication, 10. Health and Safety, 11. Personal well-being, and 12. Administrative responsibilities (86).

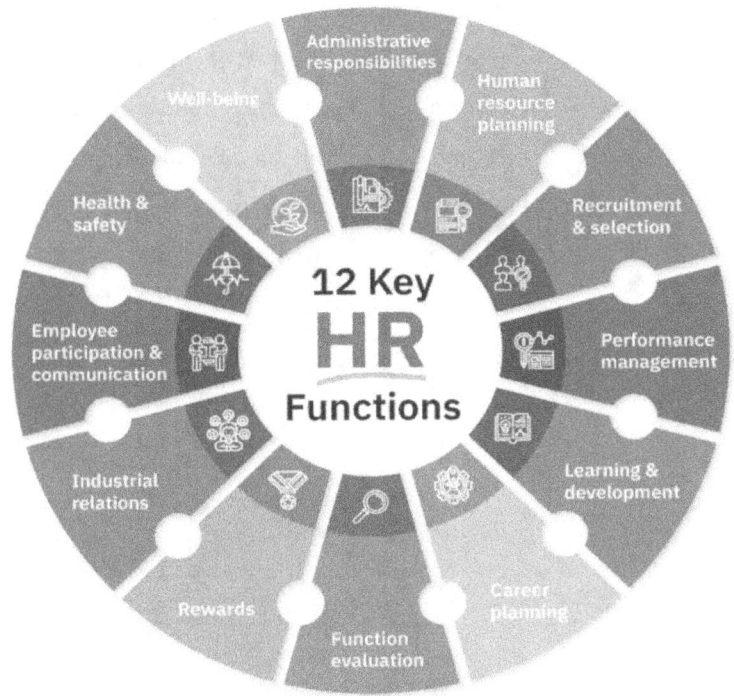

Figure 5: The Twelve Keys of Human Resource Function – Courtesy the Academy to Innovate HR (AIHR) (86).

The HR system and the delivery template constitute the HR architecture in any organization (2). The human capital characteristics, employment mode, and HR configurations constitute the HR architecture (87). Becker (2006) defines HR architecture as "The HR architecture is composed of the systems, practices, competencies, and employee performance behaviors that reflect the development and management of the firm's strategic human capital (88)." Human capital is the qualities in humans such as education, skills, intelligence, experience, and behaviors such as regularity, trustworthiness, dedication, habit, and social and personal attributes which are of economic value to an organization. These qualities differ from one individual to the other in employment and the workplace (89). Employment mode describes whether the employment is full-time or contract and the legally binding agreement in the employment. HR configuration has been described as "commitment-based, productivity-based, compliance-based, and collaborative (87)."

Human Resource System

Figure 6: Human Resource Management System – from Organization effectiveness Consultants (90).

The HR system facilitates the achievement of HR goals and is made up of HR philosophy, external environment, human capital development, internal environment, and cooperative social responsibilities. This HR system drives the HR policies, strategies, and practices.

The downstream part of the HR system is the supportive and connected HR practices shown in Figure 6.

Human resource management attention is moving from individual performance to organizational performance, which is the focus of SHRM. The human resource management system is now seen as vital to solving problems in organizations and businesses (88).

The human resource management system has been described to help in the development, planning, and determination of HR direction or strategies, HR guidelines or policies, HR procedures or processes, and HR practice of putting into effective strategies and policies (2).

The HR delivery model is the approach used by HR to make a strategic contribution to the achievement of organizational goals, provide specialist expertise, and carry out the transaction elements of HR's work such as recruitment, training, and administration.

The 'HR deliver model' also referred to as the 'HR operating model' describe the organizational structure and function with the defined task of employee and managers in terms of specified competency and implementation of designed HR policies for the organization to achieve its goals and objectives (70). The CIPD fact sheet explained it in clearer detail as "the organizational structure of HR but the roles within that structure, the capabilities required to deliver those roles, the processes within the structure, and the enablers such as technology, governance and measurement (91)."

The process to ensure business driven and well integrated HR Products and services

- Where needs, creation and implementation come together -

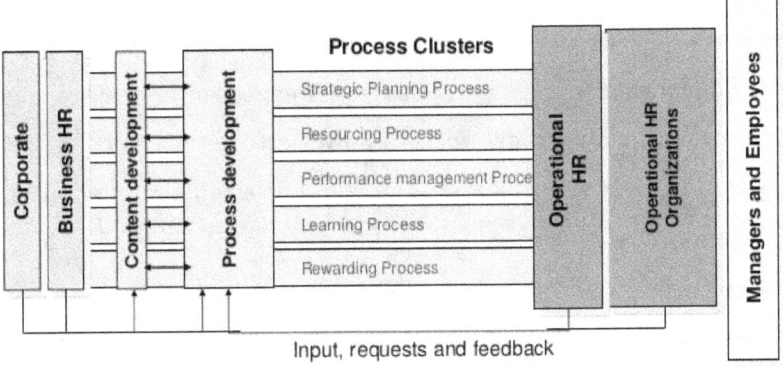

Figure 7: HR Delivery Model (92)

The concept, meaning, and nature of strategic human resource management

Organizations want to get a big slice of the market cake by using competitive strategies to woo customers and retain them as part of their business approach and initiatives by delivering values and meeting up with their expectations. This competitive strategy should be purposively designed by organizations as part of their long-term corporate strategy. Organization often achieves this competitive advantage by acting on both internal and external factors around the organization including mobilization and utilization of resources and competencies (93).

The word strategy is derived from the Greek word "strategia" which translates to literally the "art of the military commander or a military General in directing troops (94)." Strategy is necessary for uncertainty to plan to achieve organizational goals, like the military use strategy during battle to win wars (95)." Because resources are limited for an organization to achieve set goals, strategy is important to mobilize and utilize resources toward this goal. This involves determining goals and priorities, identifying action necessary, and implementing action place through mobilization and utilization of resources (96). Simeone in 2002 emphasize that "A strategy describes how the ends (goals) will be achieved by the means (resources) (97)." It is important to note that strategy may be designed purposefully or a derivation of the challenges in the operating environment of an organization to gain competitive advantage (96). It has also been seen as responsive to event or situation processes, an evolutionary or intuitive process (2). The strategy involves actions such as strategic planning and strategic thinking (98).

In the development of strategic management, it was argued that strategic decisions are the most important decisions made by management in an organization and these strategic decisions are the decisions that matter (99). The basic elements of strategic decisions of an organization which is long-term goals should include the mobilization and utilization of resources for competitive advantage and greater market shares, these elements are decisions that drive the action of the organization to achieve these goals (70). These elements include setting goals and objectives, mapping the operational environment, developing processes and establishing policies to achieve these goals, and determining and defining products and services to pursue and how to pursue these in the business enterprise. These strategic decisions must always take into cognizance what the organization will contribute or make beneficial to its stakeholders in terms of monetary or non-monetary contributions. These stakeholders in a business enterprise include customers, employees, shareholders, and actors in the external operating environments (100).

These elements also include building the core competence of the organization for competitive advantage (101,102).

Human Resources (HR) Metrics

The HR Metrics is a checklist or virtual representative tool of HR activities and functions which can help in planning, implementing, tracking, and evaluating HR activities in an organization. The HR metrics tool help in increased productivity and engagement of all stakeholders in the organization because it makes HR activities transparent. The HR metrics can also be seen as a key data point for tracking human capital utilization and how effective their human resources initiatives are in terms of measuring what is working well, what needs improvement, and what are future trends in the industry that the organization operates in. The HR matrices help the organization track its HR success (103).

The HR metrics can also be used as a virtual representation of different HR functions, processes, outputs, and outcomes. The metrics help HR teams to identify gaps, an opportunity for improvement, and areas that require more focus and attention. It includes key performance indicators

(KPIs) for each HR function such as hiring, training, performance management, employee engagement, and motivation. These are used to measure the effectiveness of each HR function or process and identify areas for improvement. Examples include i. time to fill a vacant job position, ii. Employees turnover rate, iii. The proportion of employees who completed training, iv. Employees satisfaction score, v. performance appraisal completion rate, vi. Cost per recruitment, vii. Diversity and inclusion metrics.

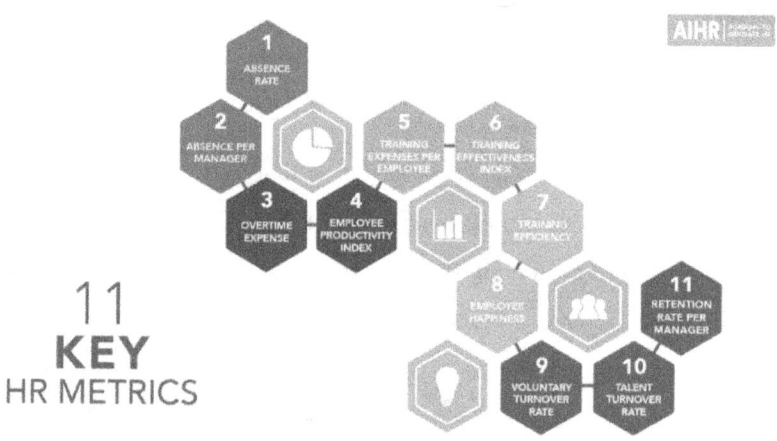

Figure 8: HR Metrics Examples – courtesy of Academy for Innovation of HR (104,105).

The HR metrics can also be used as a method of organizing the workforce of an organization into different teams based on the knowledge, skills, attitude, and experience of employees. The HR metrics framework or structure gives room for employees to work in multiple roles and on multiple projects which leads to increased utilization of talents and improved productivity in an organization.

BambooHR identified categorization of HR metrics (103):

Category 1. "HR Service and Software Metrics"

Category 2 "Recruitment Metrics"

Category 3 "Engagement and Employee Retention Metrics"

Category 4 "Time Tracking Metrics"

Category 5 "Performance Management Metrics"

Category 6 "Training and Development Metrics"

Competitive Advantage

When an organization or a company creates value for its customer, it ultimately becomes leverage for competitive advantage against competitors. This can be gained through excellence and significant shares in the market niche selected. This leverage makes a competitive advantage in such a way that it cannot be easily replicated by competitors and lead to sustainable and improved comparative advantage (106). This competitive advantage can be created by differentiation in the services and products that are unique and focusing on specific buyers or markets. Porter developed a framework of three useable strategies that organizations can use to gain competitive advantage: "innovation, quality, and cost leadership (2,106)." An organization that produces goods and services that is of good quality and produced efficiently more than its competitors will lead to the organization having a competitive advantage (55). This will lead to more sales and improve earnings and profit compared to the competitors. There are factors associated with competitive advantages like cost, structure, quality of product, distribution network, intellectual property, and customer service and branding (107). Competitive advantages are divided into two; comparative advantages and differential advantages. Comparative advantage is an organization's capability to create goods or services or value more cost-effective and efficient than a competitor, which gives the organization more market share and increases return on investment and profit. A differential advantage is when an organization produces goods or services or values that the customer sees as distinctive, matchless, and of greater quality compared to those produced by the competitors (107). The examples of these two competitive advantage are illustrated in the case studies of most capitalized company in the world at the end of this book.

The Value Chain

Porter described the value chain as the operational activities of an organization that forms part of a specialized business industry (106). The value chain is characterized by activities in an organization that are very important as well as relevant and form the basis of its unique capabilities. The objective is to gain a competitive advantage over competitors. The operational activities involved in an organization of transforming input into output is what is the value chain (108).

Porter's Value Chain Model

Figure 9: Porter's Value Chain Model

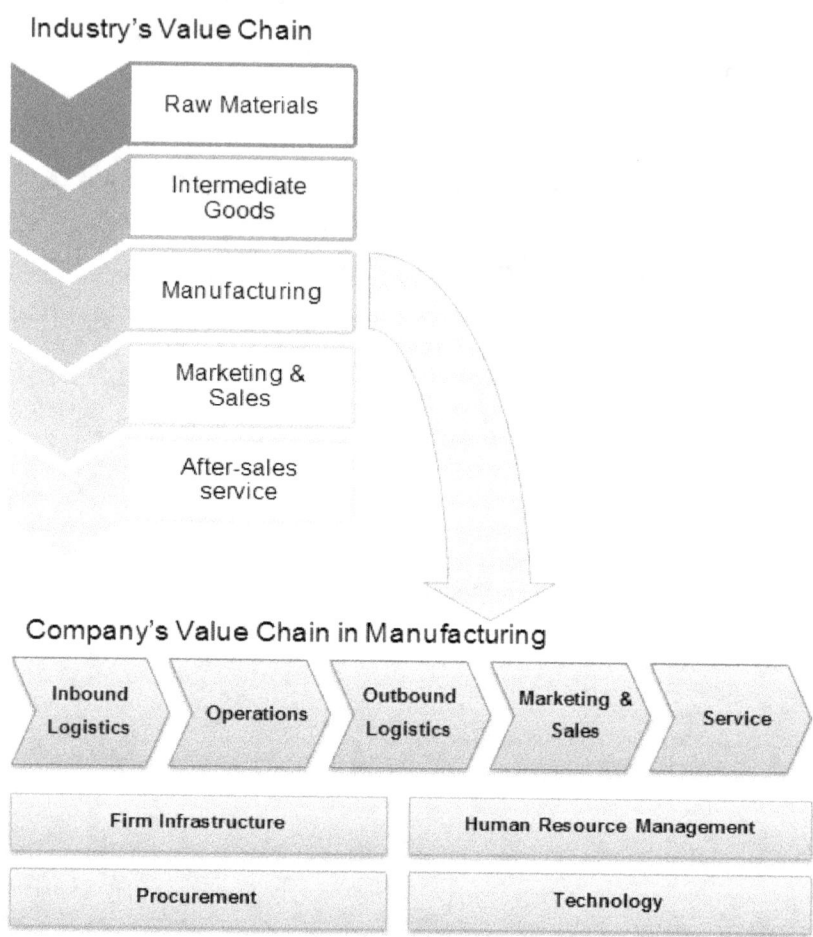

Figure 10: Transposing Industrial Value Chain to Company's Value Chain in Manufacturing (109).

The value chain is the analysis of each component of the production process into parts and operational activities (110,111). Value is gained at each activity as products are transformed at every stage of activities in the value chain order. Understanding the components of the values chain of a product or services produced by an organization is very important. Porter argued that "the chain of activities gives the products more added value than the sum of added values of all activities (106)." Porter also wrote that "Competitive advantage cannot be understood by looking at a firm as a whole. It stems from the many discrete activities a firm performs in designing, producing, marketing, delivering, and supporting its product (106)." Please see the case study of Apple Inc. to understand this explanation.

Armstrong wrote that "A value system includes the value chains of a firm's supplier (and their suppliers back to the primary supplier) and the firm itself. The value chain analysis identifies the activities of a firm and then studies the economic implications of those activities. It includes four steps: i. identify products or services as the strategic business unit, ii. identifying critical activities, iii. defining products or services, and iv. determining the value of an activity (2)."

Case Study: Apple Inc. Company Competitive advantage

Apple Inc. is a global technology company known for its innovation and high-quality products such as the iPhone, iPad, Mac, Apple Watch, and Apple TV. Through competitive advantage, the company has been successful as the most capitalized company in the world. The maintenance of these competitive advantages by Apple Inc. is through the following:

1. **Design and Innovation**: the company has a reputation to have a strong focus on product design and user experience to create user-friendly and visually appealing products

2. **Branding**: The company has created a strong brand image associated with innovation, quality, and high-end premium products to build a formidable loyal customer base that has the capacity and willingness to pay for its products.

3. **Ecosystem**: Apple products and services have an ecosystem that enables its products to function optimally. This ecosystem includes iCloud, iTunes, the Apple Store, and Apple Pay which help them to create satisfactory and seamless experiences for its customers. This is particularly important in the ability of Apple customers to be able to shift from one Apple product to another thereby increasing customer loyalty.

4. **Supply Chain Management**: This is another major factor in Apple maintaining its competitive advantage. Apple has maintained a very strong relationship with its supplier cut across the world that helps the company to implement a 'just-in-time' inventory system. This allows a quick response to changes in demand and reduces barely to the minimum, inventory cost.

5. **Retail presence**: Apple Inc. Stores had created an immense and strong retail presence for Apple to create a unique customer experience. This has allowed Apple to control its distribution channel.

6. **Maintaining High-Profit Margin**: This is another Apple competitive advantage in the intense and relentless competition in the smartphone market. This is attributable to the company's ability to charge a premium price for its product and maintain a loyal customer base.

7. **Disruption of Existing Market**: Apple has the distinctive capability to innovate and introduce new products and services that disrupt an existing market. The introduction of new products helps Apple to maintain its competitive advantage.

8. **Differentiation** This is a marketing strategy that involves creating unique products or service that is different that of competitors in a unique way. This is usually achieved through design, features, performance, quality, or other factors. This is one of Apple Inc.'s strategies for *Box 3: Apple Inc. Strategies for Competitive Advantage* maintain a competitive advantage.

9. **Innovation**

Innovation is the process of creating new ideas, products, or services that are different and better than what currently exists. Apple Inc. has been able to maintain its competitive advantage through the creation of new innovative products such as the iPhone, and iPad and has revolutionized the technology industry.

10. High Quality

High quality refers to the degree of excellence or superiority of a product or service. Apple uses high quality as one of its competitive advantages, as its products are known for high quality with attention to detail in design and manufacturing.

Distinctive Capabilities and Core Competencies

Distinctive capabilities are resources or assets that an organization uses to impact competitive advantage over its competitors that do not have these capabilities. These can be in technology, innovation, and marketing, delivering quality, and making good use of human and financial resources (2). Pralahad and Hamel defined core competencies as an organization's important and vital resource that represented the collective learning in the organization (102). When an organization evaluates itself for strengths and weaknesses and core competence to produce quality and cheaper products or services, it may gain a competitive advantage in that process over its competitors (112).

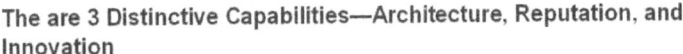

The are 3 Distinctive Capabilities—Architecture, Reputation, and Innovation

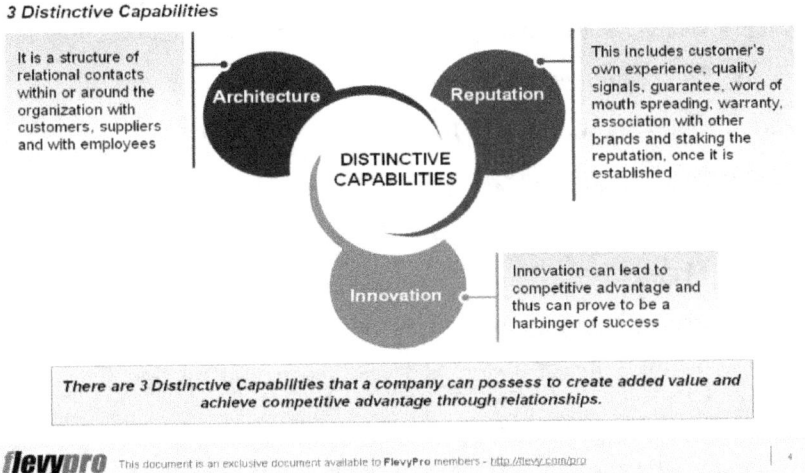

3 Distinctive Capabilities

It is a structure of relational contacts within or around the organization with customers, suppliers and with employees

Architecture

Reputation

This includes customer's own experience, quality signals, guarantee, word of mouth spreading, warranty, association with other brands and staking the reputation, once it is established

DISTINCTIVE CAPABILITIES

Innovation

Innovation can lead to competitive advantage and thus can prove to be a harbinger of success

There are 3 Distinctive Capabilities that a company can possess to create added value and achieve competitive advantage through relationships.

Figure 11: The three distinctive capabilities of an organization for competitive advantage (113).

Strategic Human Resource Management (SHRM)

Strategic human resource management (SHRM) is the complete human resource strategy accepted by the organization or business enterprises and integrated into the organization's operational and business strategies (114). Strategic human resource management has also been defined as measures put in place to integrate and align people's management to achieve organizational goals via organizationally developed human resource strategies, policies, and practices (2). Armstrong wrote that SHRM should be viewed with the following in mind:

That "*i. The human resources of an organization play a strategic role in its success; ii. HR strategies and plans should be integrated with business strategies and plans; iii. Human capital is a major source of competitive advantage; iv. It is people who implement the business strategy, and v. A systematic approach should be adopted to planning and implementing HR strategies (70).*"

Strategic Management

Strategic management stems from the organization's vision and mission and it is about the translation of these vision and mission with the articulation and implementation of the key goals and objectives. This is usually done by the managers in the organization on behalf of all the stakeholders with consideration of available resources and operating within the controls of both the internal and external environments (115). The managers in conjunction with the employees under the direction of the organization management "set objectives, analyze the internal and external environments, evaluate strategies, and share these strategies with all the stakeholders and employees within the organization (116)." To put it simply, strategic management is the articulation of the organization's objectives, setting the overall direction, developing and implementing policies, plan and allocating resources to achieve these objectives (117).

The Elements of Strategic Human Resource Management

Strategic human resources management (SHRM) was argued by Mabey et. al. as "a new way of managing? Managing performance, managing structures and employment relationships, managing to learn, managing change, and managing meaning (118)." Mabey et. al. also described three key elements of SHRM:

1. *"Internal processes of organizational change are caused or necessitated by processes of external environmental change.*

2. *Under these new environmental pressures (competition, technology, clients' demands, and so on management must develop new and appropriate strategies to defend or advance corporate interests.*

3. *This strategic response in turn requires organizational responses. If the organization is to be capable of achieving or delivering the new strategy it will be necessary to design and implement changes in any or all aspects of human resource structures and systems (18,118)."*

It is important to appreciate the following fundamental truth about SHRM by all managers that an organization or entities should hold its human resources as advantageously vital resources considering it as capital in terms of knowledge, skills, and social interactions that a worker potentially has that can be tapped into by the organization which may be the foundation for developing and implementing organization strategy (60). In addition, the organization as well should develop its human resources policies and practices that can identify, develop, and sustain the strategic capability of each worker in the organization to be able to perform optimally, this is very important in service delivery, particularly in healthcare (119).

Aims of Strategic Human Resource Management (SHRM)

The aim of SHRM is for an organization to develop innovations and flexibility through adaptability for competitive advantage in its activities and operations using its human resource. This requires strategic perspectives in the management of the organization and its human resource. The sustained competitive advantage should be the key aim of SHRM that should be achieved through continuous development of strategic capability of the organization workforce by ensuring the right mix of needed skills, commitments, and an engaged and motivated workforce (2,120,121).

Strategic human resources management should have the following objectives (121):

1. Achieve fit for purpose by integrating HR strategies with organizational strategies by fitting and alignment of the objectives of HR policies and practices to the organization's objectives and ensuring congruence of these policies and practices within the HR department.

2. Handling challenging, unpredictable, and turbulent times in both internal and external environments of the organization by HR providing stability advice, needs of both individual workers and the global needs of all operations, management, and activities, and providing strategic directions through development and timely execution of HR policies and programs.

3. Inventing ways that HR can assist with the growth and development of both individual workers and the organization as a whole and HR striving to have a direct impact on the organization's business by developing strategic roles to attract, retain and engage workers to create that long term need and competitive advantage for the organization.

Issues with the broad objectives of SHRM should include attention to ethics by taking into account all stakeholders in the organization. This consists of the employer, the employee, and the responsibility of the organization to the wider society. The corporate social responsibility of an organization is derived from the fact that the organization tap resource from the society or community and also give back resources. Corporate social responsibility (CSR) has been defined as "situations where the firm goes beyond compliance and engages in 'actions that appear to further some social good, beyond the interests of the firm and that which is required by law (122,123).'".

The Importance of Strategic Human Resources Management

The importance of SHRM includes the following:

1. The function of communicating the goals and objectives of the organization properly and well translated to the understanding of the employees. The overall strategic business direction and the role of all stakeholders in the organization for competitive advantage.

2. Identifying, attracting, and retaining employees and talents for the organization. The knowledgeable HRM department in an organization knows its employees and set goals for each employee in collaboration with the management of the organization for competitive advantage.

3. Predicting and planning for future human resources needs of the organization by helping the organization to be in operations at all times for competitive advantage.

4. Identifying, developing, adapting, and implementing different motivation measures for different categories of employees through both external and internal motivation factors identified by the HRM department including financial and non-financial motivation incentives for the organization's competitive advantage.

5. Efficient and valid performance measurement of the employee to identify the result of output for appropriate rewards and remuneration and training and education needs.

6. An integrated approach to the development and implementation of HR policies and strategies under the overall philosophy and business strategy of the organization.

7. Making all stakeholders in the organization view employees as human capital and strategic resources of the organization for competitive advantage (124,125).

Strategic human resource management is needed to address the concern about change management resulting from internal and external change environments such as culture, the need for operational efficiency and effectiveness, and improving the performance of employees for competitive advantage. It also involves predicting future needs and mobilization of resources for this after taking into consideration, the external environment, the acquisition and development of talents, and other distinctive capabilities of the organization for competitive advantage. The management of organizational development includes knowledge management, human capital development, and distinctive capabilities to improve the process of productivity in an organization (2,120).

Strategic Fit

Wikipedia describes strategic fit as an expression of *"the degree to which an organization is matching its resources and capabilities with the opportunities in the external environment. The matching takes place through strategy, and it is therefore vital that the company has the actual resources and capabilities to execute and support the strategy."* These resources can be classified as tangible (financial and physical resources) or intangible (technology like patents and copyright; human resources; reputation (brand); and culture (126).

Strategic fit has been described as related to the Resource-based view of the organization where the focus should be a close fit or alignment of human resources strategies and business strategies that are systematically designed to enhance organizational performance. The focus should also include the utilization of unique resources and capabilities of the organization for competitive advantage (127). The resource-based view emphasizes the harnessing of internal resources in an organization like HR, particularly the unique talents among employees and the unique characteristics of the organization to create a competitive advantage (2). The human resources of an organization manage the vital interdepartmental and mutually supporting operational activities and the essential external relationships.

Strategic Flexibility

Strategic flexibility has been described as the "organization's capability to identify major changes in the external environment, quickly commit resources to new courses of action in response to those changes, and recognize and act promptly when it is time to halt or reverse existing resource commitments (128)." Strategic fit and strategic flexibility should complement each other, strategic flexibility has been reported to support "innovation performance, and environmental dynamism (129)." Since most organizations operate in a dynamic, unpredictable environment, organizational development, and human capital development must emphasize developing people with a wide range of skills who can engage in a wide variety of functions for the organization (130).

Superior Performance of an Organization

It is important to emphasize that the superior performance of an organization will depend on the alignment and fit of the HR strategies with their business strategies. Delery and Doty explained that this is one of the best HR practices associated with organizational higher performance and the achievement of its goals. Their perspective on SHRM was described as a universalistic perspective, which requires that the overall organizational strategies must fit in terms of consistency of the organizational HR policies and the rest of the organization, as well as with the external environment. This universalistic perspective assumes that certain HRM practices, such as talent search, recruitment, selection, training and development, and performance management are important HR functions and effective in all organizations and can contribute to superior organizational performance when implemented correctly. They described two types of HRM practices that are essential for superior organizational performance: "internal fit and external fit. Internal fit refers to the alignment of HRM practices with each other and with the organization's goals and objectives. External fit refers to the alignment of HRM practices with the external environment, such as the industry, market, and regulator" (131). They also suggested that an organization's culture, structure, and leadership influence the effectiveness of its HR practice.

Human Resources Best Practices

Seven HR Best Practices (132) should include "i. providing security to employees, ii. Selective hiring (hiring the right people), iii. Self-managed and effective teams, iv. Fair and performance-based compensation, v. Training in relevant skills, vi. Creating a flat and egalitarian organization, and vii. Making information easily accessible to those who need it."

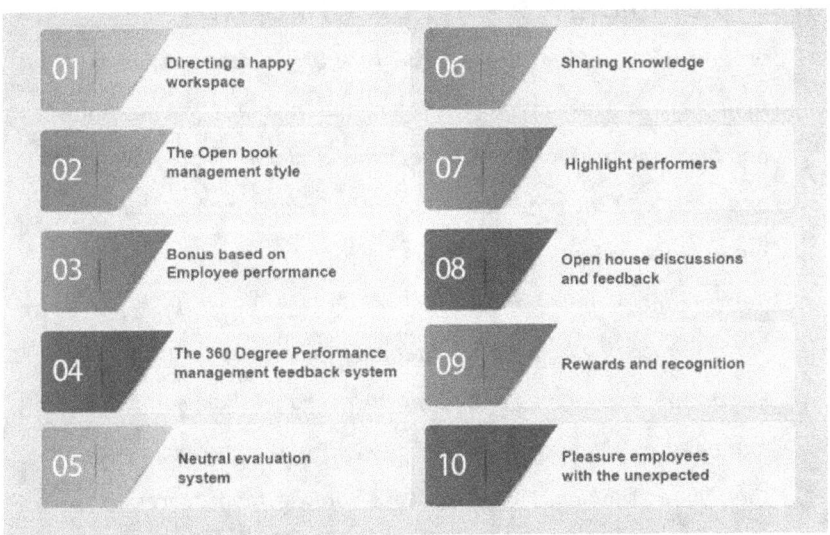

Figure 12: Top 10 HR Best Practices to Build a better workplace adapted from CuteHR (133).

Human Resource Technology Company, Empxtract.com Top Ten Recommended HR Practices (134).

1. *"1. Safe, healthy, and happy workplace*

   The organization should engage their employees and create a happy work environment, ensure employees feel comfortable and happy working for you, and make them stay for a very long time with your organization. Dig deep down into what they are thinking through the use of frequent question-and-answer sessions and surveys

2. *Open book management style*

   An organization needs to share information about the operations, structure, goals, policies, finances, and human resource make-up of the organization including what the organization is currently doing, its planning, mission, and its vision regularly. Employees should be engaged so that they feel they are an intimate part of the organization and that the success of the organization will lead to their success. Make employees interested in your strategic planning and business strategies and understand and appreciate how this fit and align with the organizational goals. Create opportunities and put in place systems for openness.

3. *Performance-linked bonuses*

   Performance of employees and teams should be measured. Performance measured and profitability should drive compensation and bonuses given to employees and which must be explained to their understanding. This should also apply to team success.

4. *360 Degree performance management feedback system*

   Every person in the organization, from management staff, managers, supervisors, and other employees must be encouraged to give feedback. This feedback system must be tailored to the performance of every team member and the response must be relevant, positive, and constructive.

5. **Fair evaluation system**

The priorities and goals of an organization should be linked to the evaluation system designed to measure individual performance. There should be a reporting relationship and self-assessment part of the evaluation system which must be clearly defined in the evaluation process. To empower the employee, evaluation should be based on achievement tracked over time. Cross-functional feedback by another manager (whose work is related and important) apart from the immediate supervisor will add to higher objectivity and fairness.

6. **Knowledge sharing**

Organization should create a database for storing knowledge that can be accessed by both the employees and the organization itself. Organizational strategies should be supported by a systematic knowledge system that empowers employees. Employees should be required to share vital knowledge and experience with others after every training and skill development program. Breakthrough and innovative ideas that are operational in the organization should be shared with employees.

7. **Highlight performers**

Reward high performers by making them visible to managers and employees through measures like putting high-performer pictures in a strategic part of the organization's office place or putting high *performers' profiles in the organization's intranet, website, etc. This creates a positive competitive environment in the organization and leads to employees putting in their best.*

8. **Open house discussions and feedback mechanism**

   Organization should create opportunities and mechanisms for a great idea that can be sourced from employees which should be identified, developed, and executed. This assists the organization to recognize and build talent and competitive advantages. The organization should create opportunities for open house discussions, staff meetings with management, and suggestion boxes and encourage staff to keep "Critical Incidents Diaries"

9. **Rewards**

   A system for talent recognition and celebration should be made public for appreciation in addition to a cash bonus. The organization should create a public forum for recognition of talent and high performance like staff award parties.

10. **Delight employees with the unexpected**

    Organization should create unexpected motivational things like rewards, gifts, or plaques. These rewards should be for top performers, employees that have stayed with the organization for a long time, and others who have shown potential."

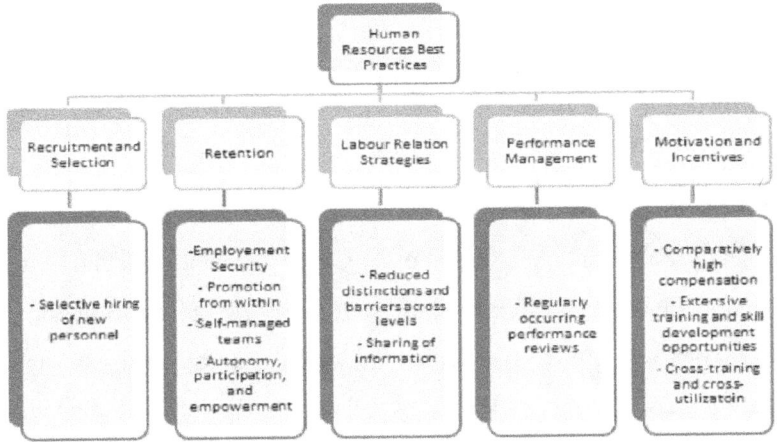

Fig 13: Human Resources Best Practice in the public sector: A conceptual framework for understanding practitioner perception of HR best practices (135).

Pfeffer (136) listed one of the renowned best HR practices: These 13 practices include

1. "Employment Security
2. Selectivity in Recruiting
3. High Wages
4. Incentive Pay
5. Employee Ownership
6. Information Sharing
7. Participation and Empowerment
8. Self-Managed Teams
9. Training and Skill Development
10. Cross-Utilization and Cross-Training

11. Symbolic Egalitarianism
12. Wage Compression
13. Promotion from Within"

The Best Fit Approach

As much as it is recommended that organizations should adopt the best practice in HRM, it is also very important that managers realize that organizations operate in a context of different internal and external environments and therefore HR policy and practices must be contingent and driven based on the circumstances and the type of organization. The best-fit approach is the practice of HRM with situational awareness of the management of an organization when integrating the HR and the organization strategies (137). That the best HR practice will be appropriate based on the context, the type of organization, its location, and the external environment in which it operates.

The Theoretical Model of Best Fit Approach - Strategic Choices

There are three theoretical models of Best Fit Approach:
1. Life-cycle model
2. Competitive Strategy
3. Strategic configuration

The Life-Cycle Model

The theoretical assumption of this model is that an organization's development has four stages: i. start-up, ii. growth, iii. maturity, and iv.

decline. This is similar to product life-cycle theory (18). The organization's HR strategies are expected to follow this cycle of change in congruence with the organizational progressive stages. Organization HR policies, programs, practices, and operations are expected to develop and change in line with the change in organizational growth and complexity (138).

Competitive Strategies and Best Fit

These three competitive strategies for consideration in terms of best fit:

1. Overall Low-Cost Provider
2. Broad Differentiation
3. Focus (Niche)

These competitive strategies should be examined under the employee's role behavior and the HR policy of the organization (139). Porter in 1985 emphasize strategies to achieve competitive advantage to include i. innovation – advancement in technology and service, ii. Quality – quality assurance and quality improvement activities and iii. Cost leadership – increasing profit by reducing cost (106).

Strategic Configuration

The impact on organizational performance is greater when HRM practices are combined in a different forms. Particularly when traditional work-based practices are combined with innovative work practices like job flexibility, employee engagement through participation in decision-making and finding solutions to problems in a team setting, training for multiple skills, employment security, etc. (140).

Conclusion

When an organization or a business enterprise or a company creates value for its customers, it ultimately becomes leverage for a competitive advantage against competitors. This is achieved through gaining excellence and significant shares in the market niche selected. This competitive advantage can be gained through SHRM. An organization's culture, structure, and leadership influence the effectiveness of its HR policy and practices for this competitive advantage. Best HRM practices and the best-fit approach are strategies that can be used in the application of HR practices by the management of an organization. The best-fit approach to HR management should be a key component of an organizational competitive strategy. Such as attracting and retaining top talent who are aligned with the organizational mission and values, investing in employee development, and promoting a diverse and inclusive workplace to ensure competitive advantage and increase productivity and profitability. The business environment that an organization operates in, and reality should always be considered in implementing HR practices, however, a contingent determination should not limit the organization in adopting HR best practices. This playbook is to guide the organization on how to develop a comprehensive HR policy that covers various aspects of employee management, including recruitment and hiring, compensation and benefits, performance management, employee engagement, and diversity and inclusion. This playbook also focused on fostering a more collaborative and innovative culture within the organization. By implementing changes to performance management, employee recognition, and talent management processes. The organization's HR policy and practices should be designed to ensure that its employees are happy and productive and that the company can continue to innovate, grow, and have a competitive advantage.

Case Studies of the most capitalized companies in the world

A case study of Amazon Inc.'s best HR practice and strategic fit

- Amazon Inc. is a global technology and e-commerce company known worldwide for its customer-centric approach, innovative business model, and operational excellence. In this case study, the analysis of Amazon HR best practices as available in the public space is presented. This case study was extracted from a report by ChatGPT, an Open AI Chatbot.

- "Amazon's best HR practices are on talent acquisition and management. The company was reported to have developed a comprehensive recruiting process that emphasizes the alignment of potential hires with the company's values and culture. This strategic fit between new hires and the company's values helps to ensure that employees are motivated, engaged, and aligned with the company's mission. These are all key elements of SHRM.

- Amazon's hiring process involves a number of steps, including an initial phone screen, a skills assessment, an interview with the hiring manager, and a final interview with a panel of senior executives. The skills assessment is designed to evaluate the candidate's technical skills, while the interviews focus on the candidate's ability to think creatively, work collaboratively, and innovate.

- Amazon's talent acquisition strategy as reported is the company's Leadership Principles, which are a set of 14 guiding principles that are used to evaluate potential hires. These principles include customer obsession, ownership, and bias for action, and are designed to ensure that new hires are aligned with the company's values and culture. The report has also shown that Amazon also places a strong emphasis on leadership development, with programmes such as the Amazon Leadership Development Program (ALDP) and the Operations Leadership Development Program (OLDP) designed to identify and develop future leaders within the company.

- Another best HR practice at Amazon is its approach to employee development. The company invests heavily in training and development programs for its employees, which are designed to help them acquire new skills and knowledge and to develop their leadership and management abilities.

- Amazon also has a unique approach to performance management, which is based on a system of continuous feedback and coaching. Managers at the company are encouraged to provide regular feedback to their employees and to work with them to identify areas of improvement and opportunities for growth. Finally, Amazon's compensation and benefits packages are designed to reward performance and to attract and retain top talent. The company offers competitive salaries, bonuses, and stock options to its employees, as well as a range of benefits, including healthcare, retirement plan, and paid leave.

- Another reported example of Amazon's best HR practice is the company's emphasis on employee engagement and retention. Amazon recognizes that engaged employees are more productive and motivated, leading to better business results. To promote employee engagement, Amazon was reported to offer a variety of perks and benefits, including health and wellness programs, flexible work schedules, and tuition reimbursement. The company also encourages employee feedback and provides opportunities for professional development, such as the Career Choice program, which provides employees with access to training and education programs.

- Amazon's HR practices are designed to ensure that employees are aligned with the company's customer-centric culture, with a focus on providing excellent service and meeting customer needs. This strategic fit has helped to drive Amazon's success, as the company has become known for its customer service and focus on delivering value to its customers.

- Overall, Amazon's focus on talent acquisition and management, employee engagement and retention, and customer obsession are examples of best HR practices that are aligned with the company's overall strategy. By focusing on developing a highly skilled and engaged workforce that is aligned with the company's values and culture, Amazon has been able to drive business success and maintain its position as a market leader.

- In summary, by investing in employee development, performance management, and compensation and benefits, the company is able to attract and retain top talent, and to create a culture of innovation and collaboration that drives its success."

Case Study 1: Amazon Inc.'s Bes HR Practice and Strategic Fit (141).

A case study of Tesla's competitive strategy using HR and best fit.

- Tesla, a leading electric vehicle manufacturer, has achieved remarkable success in the automotive industry by aligning its human resource (HR) strategy with its business strategy. In this reported case study, I will present the reported analysis of how Tesla has aligned and fit its HR strategy with its business strategy. This case study was extracted from a report by ChatGPT, an Open AI Chatbot.
- "Tesla's competitive strategy is focused on innovation and sustainability, and the company's HR practices are designed to support and reinforce this strategy. By using a Best Fit approach to HR management, Tesla is able to attract and retain top talent who share the company's values and are committed to its vision.
- One way that Tesla uses its Best Fit approach to support its competitive strategy is through its selection process. The company's hiring process is designed to identify candidates who possess the skills and characteristics that are essential for success at Tesla, such as a passion for sustainability, a willingness to take risks, and a commitment to innovation. This ensures that new hires are aligned with the company's mission and values and are able to contribute to the development of new and innovative products and technologies.
- Another way that Tesla uses its Best Fit approach is through its employee development programs. The company invests heavily in employee training and development to help employees acquire new skills and knowledge and to develop their leadership and management abilities. This not only benefits the employees but also helps Tesla to retain its top talent and to maintain a culture of innovation and collaboration.
- Tesla's Best Fit approach is also reflected in its compensation and benefits packages, which are designed to reward performance and attract and retain top talent. The

company offers competitive salaries, bonuses, and stock options, as well as a range of benefits such as healthcare, retirement plans, and paid time off. This helps to ensure that employees feel valued and are motivated to contribute to the company's success.

- Finally, Tesla's Best Fit approach supports its competitive strategy by promoting a diverse and inclusive workplace. The company has a strong commitment to creating a workplace where all employees feel valued and supported, regardless of their background or identity. This helps to attract and retain top talent from a wide range of backgrounds and perspectives, which is critical to driving innovation and sustainability.

- Overall, Tesla's Best Fit approach to HR management is a key component of the company's competitive strategy. By attracting and retaining top talent who are aligned with the company's mission and values, and by investing in employee development and promoting a diverse and inclusive workplace, Tesla is able to drive innovation and sustainability, and maintain its position as a leader in the electric vehicle and clean energy industries."

Case Study 2: A case study of Tesla's competitive strategy using HR and best-fit (141).

A case study of Microsoft's strategic HR choice and best fit

- Microsoft is a multinational technology company founded in 1975 by Bill Gates and Paul Allen. Microsoft's strategic HR choice and best fit have enabled it to become one of the most successful and influential companies in the world. In this reported case study, I present the reported analysis of Microsoft's core HR choice and best fit and how they contribute to the company's success. This case study was extracted from report by ChatGPT, an Open AI Chat bot.

- One example of Microsoft's strategic HR choice and best fit was the implementation of their "One Microsoft" strategy in 2013. This strategy aimed to break down the silos between different business units and foster collaboration across the entire organization. As part of this strategy, Microsoft made a number of HR changes that were designed to promote a more cohesive and collaborative culture.

- First, Microsoft shifted their performance management system from a traditional annual review process to a more frequent, ongoing feedback system. This allowed employees to receive regular feedback on their performance and adjust their work accordingly. Additionally, Microsoft introduced a new employee recognition program called "MyImpact," which encouraged employees to recognize and celebrate each other's contributions to the organization.

- Another HR change that Microsoft made as part of their "One Microsoft" strategy was to increase the transparency of the company's talent management process. This included implementing a new talent review system that allowed managers to review and assess the skills and potential of their employees on a regular basis. This helped to identify areas where employees needed additional training or support, as well as potential candidates for promotion or leadership position.

- Overall, Microsoft's strategic HR choices were focused on fostering a more collaborative and innovative culture within the organization. By implementing changes to their performance management, employee recognition, and talent management processes, Microsoft was able to create an environment where employees were empowered to work together and contribute to the company's success. This approach helped Microsoft to remain competitive in the rapidly evolving technology industry and position themselves as a leader in innovation and collaboration.

Case Study 3: A case study of Microsoft's strategic HR choice and best fit (141).

A case study of Alphabet Inc. employees' roles and HR policy

- Alphabet Inc. is a multinational technology company that is best known for being the parent company of Google. The company has a large and diverse workforce with employees spread across various departments and locations worldwide. This case study is to present the reported roles of Alphabet Inc. employees and company HR policies. This case study was extracted from a report by ChatGPT, an Open AI Chatbot.

- "Roles of Alphabet Inc. Employees - Alphabet Inc. has a diverse workforce that comprises various roles and positions, including but not limited to:

- Engineers: Alphabet Inc. employs a large number of engineers who work on developing new technologies and improving existing products. These engineers are responsible for designing, developing, and maintaining the company's various products and services. reach

- Marketing and Advertising Professionals: Alphabet Inc. employs a large number of marketing and advertising professionals who are responsible for promoting the company's various products and services. These professionals work on developing marketing campaigns and strategies to increase the company's visibility and reach.

- Sales Professionals: Alphabet Inc. also employs sales professionals who are responsible for selling the company's products and services to customers. These professionals work on building relationships with clients and developing sales strategies to increase revenue.
- Human Resources Professionals: Alphabet Inc. employs a team of HR professionals who are responsible for recruiting, hiring, and retaining employees. They are also responsible for developing and implementing HR policies and procedures to ensure the company's employees are happy and productive.
- HR Policies of Alphabet Inc.:
- Alphabet Inc. has a comprehensive HR policy that covers various aspects of employee management, including, but not limited to:
- Recruitment and Hiring: Alphabet Inc. has a rigorous recruitment and hiring process that ensures the company only hires the best candidates for each position. The company uses various methods to assess candidates, including interviews, aptitude tests, and technical assessments.
- Compensation and Benefits: Alphabet Inc. offers competitive compensation packages and benefits to its employees. These include health insurance, retirement plans, and stock options, among others.
- Performance Management: Alphabet Inc. has a performance management system that evaluates employees' performance on a regular basis. The company provides feedback and coaching to employees to help them improve their performance.
- Employee Engagement: Alphabet Inc. has a strong focus on employee engagement. The company provides various opportunities for employees to develop their skills and knowledge, including training programs and professional development opportunities.
- Diversity and Inclusion: Alphabet Inc. is committed to promoting diversity and inclusion in the workplace. The company has various initiatives to ensure that all employees feel valued and respected, regardless of their background or identity.
- In conclusion, Alphabet Inc. has a diverse workforce with various roles and positions. The company has a comprehensive HR policy that covers various aspects of employee management, including recruitment and hiring, compensation and benefits, performance management, employee engagement, and diversity and inclusion. The

company's HR policies are designed to ensure that its employees are happy and productive and that the company can continue to innovate and grow."

Case Study 4: A case study of Alphabet Inc. employees' roles and HR policy (141).

A case study of Meta Inc. (Facebook) strategic configuration in combining traditional work-based practice and innovative work practice

- Meta Inc. is parent company of Facebook, a social media company with a hypothetical technology company that combines traditional work-based practices and innovative work practices in order to create a productive and effective work environment. In this reported case study, I will present a reported case exploration of some of the ways in which Meta Inc. uses strategic configuration in integrating traditional and innovative practices in order to achieve its goals. This case study was extracted from a report by ChatGPT, an Open AI Chatbot.

- "One of the traditional work-based practices that Meta Inc. employs is a hierarchical organizational structure. The company has a clear chain of command, with managers and supervisors responsible for overseeing the work of their teams. This structure helps to ensure that everyone in the company knows their role and responsibilities, and it allows for clear communication and decision-making process.

- However, Meta Inc. also incorporates innovative work practices that promote collaboration and open communication. For example, the company uses an agile methodology in its software development process, which emphasizes flexibility and adaptability. This approach allows team members to work together in a more collaborative way, with regular check-ins and updates to ensure that everyone is on the same page.

- Another innovative practice that Meta Inc. employs is remote work. The company recognizes that many employees value the flexibility of being able to work from home or another location, so they have implemented a remote work policy. This allows employees to work from anywhere they choose, as long as they have a reliable internet connection.

- To support remote work and other flexible work arrangements, Meta Inc. also uses digital tools and platforms for communication and collaboration. For example, they use Slack for instant messaging and project management, and Zoom for video conferencing and virtual meetings. These tools help to keep employees connected and productive, regardless of their location.

- Overall, Meta Inc. has found success by combining traditional and innovative work practices. By using a hierarchical organizational structure, they ensure that everyone knows their role and responsibilities. However, by incorporating agile methodology, remote work, and digital tools, they are able to promote collaboration, flexibility, and productivity. This approach has helped the company to achieve its goals and remain competitive in a rapidly changing industry."

Case Study 5: A case study of Meta Inc. (Facebook) strategic configuration in combining traditional work-based practice and innovative work practice (141).

A case study of Netflix's Overall low-cost provider and HR best practice and best fit

- Netflix is a streaming service that allows subscribers to watch TV shows, movies, documentaries, and more on internet-connected devices. It was founded in 1997 by Reed Hastings and Marc Randolph and originally offered DVD rentals by mail. In 2007, the company introduced its streaming service, which has since become the main focus of its business. Today, Netflix has over 200 million subscribers in more than 190 countries and offers a wide range of original content. In this reported case study, I present a reported case study of Netflix's overall low-cost provider as a competitive strategy and best HR practice and HR best fit. This case study was extracted from a report by ChatGPT, an Open AI Chatbot.
- "Netflix is available on a variety of devices, including smartphones, tablets, smart TVs, and game consoles. Subscribers can create multiple profiles and can download content to watch offline. The service offers different subscription plans, with different features and pricing
- Netflix has been able to successfully differentiate itself from its competitors by offering a low-cost provider strategy, which allows it to provide a large library of TV shows and movies at affordable prices. At the same time, the company has also implemented a number of innovative HR best practices that have contributed to its success. In this case study, we will explore how Netflix has leveraged its low-cost

provider strategy and HR best practices to become one of the most successful entertainment companies in the world.

Low-Cost Provider Strategy:

Netflix's low-cost strategy is built on several key elements:

- Low-Cost Structure: Netflix operates on a lean business model that minimizes overhead costs. By using a digital platform to distribute its content, the company is able to avoid the high costs associated with traditional media distribution methods.
- Large and Diverse Content Library: Netflix has invested heavily in creating a vast and diverse content library, which includes a mix of licensed and original programming. This has allowed the company to attract a large and diverse customer base.
- Pricing Strategy: Netflix has been able to offer its services at a low price point by offering a variety of pricing tiers to its customers. By allowing customers to choose the plan that best fits their needs and budget, Netflix has been able to build a loyal customer base.

HR Best Practices:

Netflix has also implemented a number of innovative HR best practices that have contributed to its success:

- Freedom and Responsibility: Netflix has a unique culture that values freedom and responsibility. The company encourages employees to take ownership of their work and make decisions independently. This approach has allowed the company to move quickly and respond to market changes in a timely manner
- No Formal Performance Reviews: Netflix does not have a formal performance review process. Instead, the company expects managers to provide ongoing feedback and coaching to employees. This approach fosters a culture of continuous learning and improvement.
- Generous Employee Benefits: Netflix offers generous employee benefits, including unlimited vacation time and parental leave. This has helped the company attract and retain top talent in a highly competitive industry.

Best Fit:

Netflix's low-cost provider strategy and HR best practices are highly aligned with the company's overall business strategy. By operating on a lean business model and offering affordable pricing, the company is able to attract a large and diverse customer base. At the same time, the company's unique culture and approach to HR management have helped it build a high-performing team of employees who are able to innovate and respond to market changes quickly.

In conclusion, Netflix's low-cost provider strategy and HR best practices have been instrumental in the company's success. By offering affordable pricing and a vast and diverse content library, Netflix has been able to build a large and loyal customer base. And by fostering a culture of freedom and responsibility and offering generous employee benefits, the company has been able to attract and retain top talent."

Case Studies 6:A Case studies of Netflix's overall low-cost provider as a competitive strategy and best HR practice and HR best fit (141).

A case study of YouTube overall low cost provider as a competitive strategy and best HR practice and HR best fit

- YouTube is an online video-sharing platform that was founded in 2005. The platform has grown rapidly over the years and is now the second-largest search engine in the world, after Google. Reports has shown that YouTube has been able to maintain its position as a leading platform by using a low-cost provider and implementing HR best practices. In this reported case study, this is to present a reported case study of YouTube overall low-cost provider as a competitive strategy and best HR practice and HR best fit. This case study was extracted from report by ChatGPT, an Open AI Chat bot.

- "Low-Cost Provider Strategy: YouTube has been able to maintain its position as a leading platform by using a low-cost provider strategy. The platform offers a free service to its users, which has been a key factor in its growth. YouTube is able to keep its costs low by using technology to automate many of its processes. The platform uses algorithms to recommend videos to users and to target advertisements to specific audiences. This has allowed YouTube to scale its operations quickly and efficiently while keeping cost low.

- HR Best Practices: YouTube's success can also be attributed to its HR best practices. The platform has a strong culture of innovation and collaboration, which has helped it to attract and retain top talent. YouTube offers its employees a range of benefits, including free meals, onsite gyms, and generous vacation policies. The platform also encourages its employees to take risks and experiment with new idea.

- HR Best Fit: YouTube's HR practices are well-aligned with its low-cost provider strategy. The platform's culture of innovation and experimentation allows it to continuously improve its technology and processes, which helps to keep costs low. Additionally, YouTube's generous benefits packages and supportive work environment help to attract and retain top talent, which is essential for maintaining the platform's competitive position.

- In conclusion, YouTube's low-cost provider strategy and HR best practices have been instrumental in the platform's success. The company has been able to maintain its position as a leading platform by using technology to automate many of its processes and by offering a supportive work environment that attracts and retains top talent. This has helped YouTube to keep its cost low while continuing to innovate and grow."

Case Studies 7: Case studies of YouTube's overall low-cost provider as a competitive strategy and best HR practice and HR best fit (141).

A case study of Nvidia Inc.'s broad differentiation and HR best fit

- Nvidia Inc. is a technology company that specializes in designing graphics processing units (GPUs) for a variety of industries, including gaming, data center, professional visualization, and artificial intelligence. One of the key factors that set Nvidia apart from its competitors is its focus on broad differentiation, which includes the development of cutting-edge technology and a commitment to providing exceptional customer service. In this reported case study, I present a reported case study of Nvidia Inc.'s broad differentiation and HR best fit.. This case study was extracted from a report by ChatGPT, an Open AI Chatbot.

- "In order to achieve broad differentiation, Nvidia has also implemented HR best-fit strategies that align with its business goals. One example of this is the company's approach to recruitment and selection. Nvidia places a strong emphasis on hiring individuals who possess the necessary skills and experience to excel in their roles, as well as those who share the company's values and commitment to innovation. This approach ensures that Nvidia is able to attract and retain top talent in the industry, which is critical for maintaining its competitive advantage.

- Another example of Nvidia's HR best-fit strategies is its approach to employee development. The company offers a range of training programs and professional development opportunities that are tailored to the needs of its employees and designed to help them stay up to date with the latest industry trends and technologies. By investing in its employees in this way, Nvidia is able to foster a culture of innovation and creativity, which is critical for maintaining its position as a market leader.

- Nvidia's commitment to HR best fit is also reflected in its employee benefits and compensation packages. The company offers a range of benefits, including comprehensive health insurance, retirement plans, and stock options, that are designed to attract and retain top talent. Additionally, Nvidia offers competitive salaries that are based on the skills and experience of each individual employee, which ensures that the company is able to attract and retain the best talent in the industry.

- In summary, Nvidia's commitment to broad differentiation and HR best fit is a key factor in its success as a technology company. By investing in its employees and ensuring that its HR policies align with its business goals, Nvidia has created a culture of innovation and excellence that is critical for maintaining its position as a market leader."

Case Study 8: A case study of Nvidia Inc.'s broad differentiation and HR best fit (141).

A case study of Saudi Aramco focus on niche market and HR best practice and HR best fit

- Saudi Aramco is a multinational oil and gas company based in Saudi Arabia, and it is the world's largest oil company. The company has a significant presence in the global oil and gas industry, and it has a strong focus on niche markets. In addition, Saudi Aramco is known for its best HR practices and the use of HR best fit to ensure that its employees are motivated, engaged, and productive. In this reported case study, I present a reported case study of Saudi Aramco focus on niche market and HR best practice and HR best fit. This case study was extracted from report by ChatGPT, an Open AI Chat bot.

- "Niche Markets: Saudi Aramco has a strong focus on niche markets, which has helped it to become a leader in the oil and gas industry. The company has identified specific areas where it can excel, such as offshore oil drilling and oil exploration, and has invested heavily in these areas. This focus on niche markets has allowed Saudi Aramco to differentiate itself from other oil companies and establish a competitive advantage in the industry.

- HR Best Practices: Saudi Aramco is known for its best HR practices, which include a focus on employee engagement, development, and retention. The company has a comprehensive performance management system that helps to ensure that its employees are performing at their best. In addition, Saudi Aramco provides extensive training and development programs to help its employees develop their skills and advance in their careers.

- HR Best Fit: Saudi Aramco also uses HR best fit to ensure that its employees are motivated and engaged. The company recognizes that different employees have different needs, and it tailors its HR practices to meet those needs. For example, Saudi Aramco has a flexible work arrangement program that allows employees to work from home or work flexible hours to accommodate their personal needs.

- In conclusion, Saudi Aramco's focus on niche markets, best HR practices, and HR best fit has helped the company to become a leader in the oil and gas industry. By investing in its employees and tailoring its HR practices to meet their needs, Saudi Aramco has been able to attract and retain top talent, which has contributed to its success."

Case Study 9: A case study of Saudi Aramco focuses on a niche market and HR best Practices and HR best fit (141)

References

1. SHRM [Internet]. 2021 [cited 2021 Jul 19]. Practicing Strategic Human Resources. Available from: https://www.shrm.org/resourcesandtools/tools-and-samples/toolkits/pages/practicingstrategichumanresources.aspx

2. Armstrong M. Armstrong's Handbook of Strategic Human Resource Management: Improve Business Performance Through Strategic People Management. 7th edition. London⬚; New York: Kogan Page; 2020. 312 p.

3. Storey J. Human Resource Management A Critical Text: A Critical Text. 3rd edition. London: Cengage Learning; 2007. 312 p.

4. Becker BE, Ulrich D, Huselid MA. The HR Scorecard: Linking People, Strategy, and Performance. 1st edition. Harvard Business Review Press; 2001. 273 p.

5. Ulrich D, Brockbank W. The HR Value Proposition. 1st edition. Harvard Business Review Press; 2005. 338 p.

6. Beaven K. Strategic Human Resource Management: An HR Professional's Toolkit. 1st edition. London: Kogan Page; 2019. 272 p.

7. Boxall P. The Strategic Hrm Debate and the Resource-Based View of the Firm. Hum Resour Manag J. 1996;6(3):59–75.

8. Shani N, Divyapriya P, Logesshnavi K. HUMAN RESOURCE PHILOSOPHY. Int J Manag IJM. 2011;2(1):61–8.

9. Kuimov V. A Contextual-Functional Analysis of the Enterprise Performance. Int J Entrep Behav Res. 2017 Jan 1;23(2):356–62.

10. Functional Analysis of Business Activities at Tesla – Michael Nelson [Internet]. [cited 2022 Dec 21]. Available from: https://omnelson.com/2020/12/functional-analysis-of-business-activities-at-tesla

11. Tolan J. This Elon Musk Philosophy Will Forever Change Your Hiring Process [Internet]. Human Resources Blog - Spark Hire. 2018 [cited 2022 Dec 21]. Available from: https://hr.sparkhire.com/best-hiring-practices/elon-musk-change-your-hiring-process/

12. Global Data. Tesla Inc: Overview. 2022 [cited 2022 Dec 21]. Tesla Inc Company Profile - Overview. Available from: https://www.globaldata.com/company-profile/tesla-inc/

13. Lordkipanidze R. Potentiality and Benefits from Apple Production. 2019.

14. Global Data. Apple Inc Company Profile - Apple Inc Overview [Internet]. [cited 2022 Dec 21]. Available from: https://www.globaldata.com/company-profile/apple-inc/

15. Sharma V, Sharma J. Organisational Innovation through HR Practices: A Review Based Analysis. 2018.

16. Source Essay Writing Service. HR Strategy At Apple Make Their Employees Creative And Innovative [Internet]. Online essay writing service. 2020 [cited 2022 Dec 21]. Available from: https://sourceessay.com/hr-strategy-at-apple-make-their-employees-creative-and-innovative/

17. Meyer J, Allen N. Commitment in the Workplace: Theory, Research, and Application [Internet]. Thousand Oaks, California; 1997 [cited 2021 Jul 28]. Available from: https://sk.sagepub.com/books/commitment-in-the-workplace

18. Armstrong M. Armstrong's Handbook of Strategic Human Resource Management. Fifth edition. London⊡; Philadelphia: Kogan Page; 2011. 328 p.

19. Meyer JP, Allen NJ. A three-component conceptualization of organizational commitment. Hum Resour Manag Rev. 1991 Mar 1;1(1):61–89.

20. Meyer JP, Stanley DJ, Herscovitch L, Topolnytsky L. Affective, Continuance, and Normative Commitment to the Organization: A Meta-analysis of Antecedents, Correlates, and Consequences. J Vocat Behav. 2002 Aug 1;61(1):20–52.

21. Ćulibrk J, Delić M, Mitrović S, Ćulibrk D. Job Satisfaction, Organizational Commitment and Job Involvement: The Mediating Role of Job Involvement. Front Psychol [Internet]. 2018 [cited 2022 Dec 21];9. Available from: https://www.frontiersin.org/articles/10.3389/fpsyg.2018.00132

22. Luthans F, Luthans BC, Luthans KW. Organizational Behavior: An Evidence-Based Approach, 13th Ed. Illustrated edition. Charlotte, North Carolina: Information Age Publishing; 2015. 536 p.

23. Khan H, Rehmat M, Butt TH, Farooqi S, Asim J. Impact of transformational leadership on work performance, burnout and social loafing: a mediation model. Future Bus J. 2020 Dec 9;6(1):40.

24. McLeod S. Simply Psychology. 2023 [cited 2023 Mar 25]. Albert Bandura's Social Learning Theory - Simply Psychology. Available from: https://simplypsychology.org/bandura.html

25. Bandura A. Social learning theory. Oxford, England: Prentice-Hall; 1977. viii, 247 p. (Social learning theory).

26. Akers RL, Jennings WG. 21st Century Criminology: A Reference Handbook. In: 21st Century Criminology: A Reference Handbook [Internet]. Thousand Oaks: SAGE Publications, Inc.; 2009 [cited 2023 Mar 25]. p. 323–31. Available from: https://sk.sagepub.com/reference/criminology/n37.xml

27. Maisto SA, Carey KB, Bradizza CM. Social learning theory. In: Psychological theories of drinking and alcoholism, 2nd ed. New York, NY, US: The Guilford Press; 1999. p. 106–63. (The Guilford substance abuse series).

28. Adams JS. Inequity In Social Exchange. In: Berkowitz L, editor. Advances in Experimental Social Psychology [Internet]. Academic Press; 1965 [cited 2023 Mar 25]. p. 267–99. Available from: https://www.sciencedirect.com/science/article/pii/S0065260108601082

29. Daugherty G. Investopedia. 2023 [cited 2023 Mar 25]. What Is Quiet Quitting—and Is It a Real Trend? Available from: https://www.investopedia.com/what-is-quiet-quitting-6743910

30. Pritchard RD. Equity theory: A review and critique. Organ Behav Hum Perform. 1969 May 1;4(2):176–211.

31. Adams JS, Freedman S. Equity Theory Revisited: Comments and Annotated Bibliography. In: Berkowitz L, Walster E, editors. Advances in Experimental Social Psychology [Internet]. Academic Press; 1976 [cited 2023 Mar 25]. p. 43–90. Available from: https://www.sciencedirect.com/science/article/pii/S0065260108600581

32. McGregor D. The human side of enterprise. New York: McGraw-Hill; 1960. 246 p. (Penguin business library).

33. Lawter L, Kopelman RE, Prottas DJ. McGregor's theory X/Y and job performance: A multilevel, multi-source analysis. J Manag Issues. 2015;27:84–101.

34. Nikolopoulou K. Scribbr. 2022 [cited 2023 Mar 25]. What Is the Hawthorne Effect? | Definition & Examples. Available from: https://www.scribbr.com/research-bias/hawthorne-effect/

35. Wickström G, Bendix T. The "Hawthorne effect"--what did the original Hawthorne studies actually show? Scand J Work Environ Health. 2000 Aug;26(4):363–7.

36. Sedgwick P, Greenwood N. Understanding the Hawthorne effect. BMJ. 2015 Sep 4;351:h4672.

37. Scientific management. In: Wikipedia [Internet]. 2023 [cited 2023 Mar 25]. Available from: https://en.wikipedia.org/w/index.php?title=Scientific_management&oldid=1134038085

38. Taylor FW. The Principles of Scientific Management. Mineola, N.Y: Dover Publications; 1997. 80 p.

39. Maslow AH, Press G. A Theory of Human Motivation. GENERAL PRESS; 2019. 60 p.

40. Expectancy theory. In: Wikipedia [Internet]. 2023 [cited 2023 Mar 26]. Available from: https://en.wikipedia.org/w/index.php?title=Expectancy_theory&oldid=1143784187

41. Oliver RL. Expectancy Theory Predictions of Salesmen's Performance. J Mark Res. 1974 Aug 1;11(3):243–53.

42. Vroom VH. Work and motivation. Oxford, England: Wiley; 1964. (Work and motivation).

43. Wabba MA, House RJ. Expectancy Theory in Work and Motivation: Some Logical and Methodological Issues. Hum Relat. 1974 Feb 1;27(2):121–47.

44. Reeve J. Understanding Motivation and Emotion. 5th edition. Hoboken, NJ: Wiley; 2008. 600 p.

45. Clements-Croome D, editor. Creating the Productive Workplace: Places to Work Creatively. 3rd edition. London⍰: New York: Routledge; 2017. 466 p.

46. Marin-Garcia JA, Tomas JM. Deconstructing AMO framework: a systematic review. Intang Cap. 2016 Sep 22;12(4):1040–87.

47. Appelbaum E, Bailey T, Berg P, Kalleberg AL. Manufacturing Advantage: Why High Performance Work Systems Pay Off. Ithaca: ILR Press; 1999. 304 p.

48. Bailey T, Berg P, Sandy C. The Effect of High-Performance Work Practices on Employee Earnings in the Steel, Apparel, and Medical Electronics and Imaging Industries. ILR Rev. 2001 Mar 1;54(2A):525–43.

49. John Purcell Peter Boxall JP. Strategy and Human Resource Management. Palgrave Macmillan; 2002.

50. Zhu C, Liu A, Chen G. High performance work systems and corporate performance: the influence of entrepreneurial orientation and organizational learning. Front Bus Res China. 2018 Feb 28;12(1):4.

51. Snell S. Principles of Human Resource Management. by Scott Snell, George Bohlander. International ed of 16th revised ed edition. Mason, Ohio: Thomson South-Western; 2012.

52. McCracken M, McIvor R, Treacey R, Wall T. Human capital theory: assessing the evidence for value and importance of

people to aorganization sucess [Internet]. London: Chartered Institute of Personnel and Development (CIPD) and Ulster University Business School; 2017 May [cited 2021 Jul 31]. Available from: https://www.cipd.co.uk/Images/human-capital-theory-assessing-the-evidence_tcm18-22292.pdf

53. Schuler RS, Jackson SE, editors. Strategic Human Resource Management. 2nd edition. Malden, MA: Wiley-Blackwell; 2007. 498 p.

54. Lado AA. Review of Strategic Human Resource Management. Acad Manage Rev. 2000;25(3):677–9.

55. Barney JB, Hesterly WS. Strategic Management and Competitive Advantage: Concepts. 4th ed. edition. Upper Saddle River, N.J: Prentice Hall; 2011. 377 p.

56. Barney JB, Clark DN. Resource-Based Theory: Creating and Sustaining Competitive Advantage. Illustrated edition. Oxford⬚; New York: Oxford University Press; 2007. 350 p.

57. Fiedler FE. Leadership Effectiveness. Am Behav Sci. 1981 May 1;24(5):619–32.

58. Donaldson L. The Contingency Theory of Organizations. 1st edition. Thousand Oaks, Calif: SAGE Publications, Inc; 2001. 344 p.

59. Luthans F, Stewart TI. A General Contingency Theory of Management. Acad Manage Rev. 1977;2(2):181–95.

60. Boxall P. High-performance work systems: what, why, how and for whom? Asia Pac J Hum Resour. 2012;50(2):169–86.

61. Collings DG, Wood GT, Szamosi LT, editors. Human Resource Management: A Critical Approach. 2nd ed. London: Routledge; 2018. 450 p.

62. Storey J, Ulrich D, Wright P. Strategic Human Resource Management. 1st edition. S.l.: Routledge; 2020. 120 p.

63. Beer M, Spector B, Lawrence PR, Mills DQ, Walton RE. Managing Human Assets. New York⊠: London: The Free Press; 1984. 209 p.

64. Fombrun, DEVANNA, TICHY. Strategic Human Resource Management. New York: John Wiley & Sons; 1984. 520 p.

65. Legge K. Human Resource Management: Rhetorics and Realities. 2004th edition. Houndmills, Basingstoke, Hampshire⊠; New York, N.Y: Red Globe Press; 2004. 448 p.

66. Guest DE. Human Resource Management and Industrial Relations[1]. J Manag Stud. 1987;24(5):503–21.

67. Storey J. Developments in the Management of Human Resources: An Analytical Review. Blackwell Publishers; 1992. 304 p.

68. Storey J. New Perspectives on Human Resource Management (Routledge Revivals). London: Routledge; 2014. 222 p.

69. Bailey C, Gratton L, Hope-Hailey V, McGovern P, Stiles P. Soft and Hard Models of Human Resource Management: A Reappraisal. J Manag Stud. 1997 Jan 1;34.

70. Armstrong M. Armstrong's Handbook of Strategic Human Resource Management [Internet]. Fifth. London⊠; Philadelphia: Kogan Page; 2011 [cited 2021 Jul 19]. 328 p. Available from: https://www.koganpage.com/product/armstrong-s-handbook-of-strategic-human-resource-management-9781789661729

71. BrightHR. Hard and Soft HRM. 2020 [cited 2023 Mar 27]. hard-and-soft-hrm. Available from: https://www.brighthr.com/articles/hris/hard-and-soft-hrm/

72.   whatishumanresource. Whatishumanresource.com - Human Resource Management - What is HRM? - Definitions - Functions - Objectives - Importance - Evolution of HRM from Personnel management [Internet]. 2023 [cited 2023 Mar 26]. Available from: https://www.whatishumanresource.com/human-resource-management

73.   Association for Talent Development A. Talent development glossary terms. [cited 2023 Apr 2]. What is Organization Development | The 5 Phases of OD Strategies | ATD. Available from: http://en.atdchina.com.cn/talent-development-glossary-terms/what-is-organization-development

74.   Wikipedia. Industrial relations. In: Wikipedia [Internet]. 2022 [cited 2023 Apr 3]. Available from: https://en.wikipedia.org/w/index.php?title=Industrial_relations&oldid=1111306597

75.   Baruah S. Nurture an Engaged and Satisfied Workforce | Vantage Circle HR Blog. 2023 [cited 2023 Apr 3]. Employee Engagement: Creating A Engaging Work Culture. Available from: https://blog.vantagecircle.com/employee-engagement/

76.   Indeed Editorial Team. Indeed Career Guide. 2023 [cited 2023 Apr 3]. How To Improve Employee Relations in 5 Steps (With Benefits) | Indeed.com. Available from: https://www.indeed.com/career-advice/career-development/improve-employee-relations

77.   International Labour Organization I. Industrial and employment relations (GOVERNANCE) [Internet]. [cited 2023 Apr 3]. Available from: https://www.ilo.org/ifpdial/areas-of-work/industrial-and-employment-relations/lang--en/index.htm

78.   Babal S. hrnxt Performance and Productivity. 2020 [cited 2023 Apr 4]. How Tesla step-up its HR game? | hrnxt.com. Available

from: https://hrnxt.com/hr/how-tesla-step-up-its-hr-game/14488/2020/02/14/

79. TESLA. Tesla Anti-Handbook Handbook | PDF [Internet]. 2020 [cited 2023 Apr 4]. Available from: https://www.scribd.com/document/446927426/Tesla-Anti-Handbook-Handbook?secret_password=tL7xWs12RWRhuakJfoYs#fullscreen&from_embed

80. Bock T. What is Driver Analysis? [Internet]. Displayr. 2018 [cited 2023 Apr 4]. Available from: https://www.displayr.com/what-is-driver-analysis/

81. Quantum Workplace. Employee Engagement Software | Quantum Workplace [Internet]. 2023 [cited 2023 Apr 4]. Available from: https://www.quantumworkplace.com/product/employee-engagement-software

82. Friedman J. Why Employee Engagement Is Important: 16 Benefits [Internet]. Emeritus Online Courses. 2022 [cited 2023 Apr 4]. Available from: https://emeritus.org/blog/why-employee-engagement-is-important-benefits/

83. Indeed Editorial Team. Indeed Career Guide. 2022 [cited 2023 Apr 4]. Diversity and Inclusiveness: Definition, Benefits and Guide. Available from: https://au.indeed.com/career-advice/career-development/diversity-and-inclusiveness

84. Mainwaring S. Forbes. 2021 [cited 2023 Apr 5]. Purpose At Work: How Google Is Building Diversity And Inclusion With Performance Paradigm. Available from: https://www.forbes.com/sites/simonmainwaring/2021/06/28/purpose-at-work-how-google-is-building-diversity--inclusion-with-performance-paradigm/

85. Bush M. Great Place To Work®. [cited 2023 Apr 4]. Why Is Diversity & Inclusion in the Workplace Important? Available from: https://www.greatplacetowork.com/resources/blog/why-is-diversity-inclusion-in-the-workplace-important

86. Vulpen E van. Academy to Innovate HR (AIHR). 2023 [cited 2023 Mar 26]. The 12 Key Functions of Human Resources. Available from: https://www.aihr.com/blog/human-resources-functions/

87. Lepak DP, Snell SA. Examining the Human Resource Architecture: The Relationships Among Human Capital, Employment, and Human Resource Configurations. J Manag. 2002 Aug 1;28(4):517–43.

88. Becker BE, Huselid MA. Strategic Human Resources Management: Where Do We Go From Here? J Manag. 2006 Dec 1;32(6):898–925.

89. Kenton W. Investopedia. [cited 2021 Jul 28]. Human Capital. Available from: https://www.investopedia.com/terms/h/humancapital.asp

90. Organization Effectiveness Consultants. OEC STRATEGIC SOLUTIONS. 2020 [cited 2023 Jul 29]. Human Resources Model. Available from: https://oecstrategicsolutions.com/wp-content/uploads/2017/02/Human-Resources-Model.png

91. Chartered Institute of Personnel Development C. Changing HR Operating Models [Internet]. London: Chartered Institute of Personnel and Development (CIPD) and Ulster University Business School; 2015 Feb [cited 2021 Aug 3]. (A collection of thought pieces). Available from: https://www.cipd.co.uk/knowledge/strategy/hr/operating-models

92. Peyman Dayyani. HR Service Delivery Model [Internet]. 11:38:31 UTC [cited 2021 Aug 3]. Available from: https://www.slideshare.net/pdayyani/hr-service-delivery-model

93. Whittington R. Johnson: Exploring Strategy TO p12. 2020.

94. Wikipedia. Strategy. In: Wikipedia [Internet]. 2021 [cited 2021 Aug 18]. Available from: https://en.wikipedia.org/w/index.php?title=Strategy&oldid=10 29729251

95. Greene R. The 33 Strategies of War. Reprint edition. London: Penguin Books; 2007. 512 p.

96. Freedman L, Murray MB, Studios A. Strategy: A History.

97. Simeone L. Characterizing Strategic Design Processes in Relation to Definitions of Strategy from Military, Business and Management Studies. Des J. 2020 Jul 3;23(4):515–34.

98. Mintzberg H, Quinn JB. The Strategy Process: Concepts, Context and Cases. Subsequent edition. Upper Saddle River, N.J: Pearson College Div; 1995. 990 p.

99. Drucker PF. The Practice of Management. Reissue edition. New York: Harper Business; 2006. 416 p.

100. Chandler JAD. Strategy and Structure: Chapters in the History of the American Industrial Enterprise. Washington, D.C: Beard Books; 1962. 480 p.

101. Hahn D, Taylor B, editors. Strategic Business Planning - Strategic Business Management: Status and development trends [Internet]. 9th ed. Berlin Heidelberg: Springer-Verlag; 2006 [cited 2021 Aug 19]. Available from: https://www.springer.com/gp/book/9783540235750

102. Prahalad CK, Hamel G. The Core Competence of the Corporation. Harv Bus Rev. 1990;14.

103. Fica T. BambooHR People, data, and analytics. 2023 [cited 2023 Apr 7]. The 29 Most Important HR Metrics You Need to Track. Available from: https://www.bamboohr.com/blog/key-hr-metrics

104. Vulpen E van. 14 HR Metrics Examples [Internet]. AIHR. 2016 [cited 2023 Apr 7]. Available from: https://www.aihr.com/blog/14-hr-metrics-examples/

105. Vulpen E van. 11 Key HR Metrics [Internet]. AIHR. 2016 [cited 2023 Jul 29]. Available from: https://www.aihr.com/blog/11-key-hr-metrics/

106. Porter ME. Competitive advantage: creating and sustaining superior performance. New York: London: Free Press; Collier Macmillan; 1985. 557 p.

107. Alexandra Twin. Investopedia. [cited 2021 Aug 23]. Competitive Advantage: What Gives Companies an Edge. Available from: https://www.investopedia.com/terms/c/competitive_advantage.asp

108. Grant RM. Contemporary Strategy Analysis Text Only. 9th edition. Chichester, West Sussex, UK; Hoboken: Wiley; 2016. 480 p.

109. Jurevicius O. Strategic Management Insight. 2013 [cited 2021 Aug 23]. Looking at your Value Chain will make you Smarter. Available from: https://www.strategicmanagementinsight.com/tools/value-chain-analysis.html

110. Kay J. Foundations of Corporate Success: How Business Strategies Add Value. 1st edition. Oxford: Oxford University Press; 2003. 416 p.

111. Kay J. The Structure of Strategy. Bus Strategy Rev. 1993;4(2):17–37.

112. The Macat Team. An Analysis of C.K. Prahalad and Gary Hamel's The Core Competence of the Corporation. 1st edition. Macat Library; 2017. 111 p.

113. FlevyPro. Distinctive Capabilities Framework (17-slide PowerPoint presentation (PPT)) - FlevyPro Document | Flevy [Internet]. 2016 [cited 2023 Apr 7]. Available from: https://flevy.com/browse/flevypro/distinctive-capabilities-framework-2657

114. Purcell PBJ. Strategy and Human Resource Management. 2 edition. Palgrave Macmillan; 2007.

115. Wikipedia. Strategic management. In: Wikipedia [Internet]. 2021 [cited 2021 Aug 28]. Available from: https://en.wikipedia.org/w/index.php?title=Strategic_management&oldid=1037575348

116. Kenton W. Investopedia. [cited 2021 Aug 28]. How Strategic Management Works. Available from: https://www.investopedia.com/terms/s/strategic-management.asp

117. Ayitey W. A Simple Approach to Strategic Management. 2010.

118. Mabey C, Salaman G, Storey J. Human Resource Management: A Strategic Introduction. 2nd edition. Oxford, UK◻; Malden, Mass., USA: Wiley-Blackwell; 1998. 604 p.

119. Kabene SM, Orchard C, Howard JM, Soriano MA, Leduc R. The importance of human resources management in health care: a global context. Hum Resour Health. 2006 Jul 27;4(1):20.

120. Boxall P, Purcell J, Wright P. The Oxford Handbook of Human Resource Management [Internet]. The Oxford Handbook of Human Resource Management. Oxford University Press; 2008 [cited 2021 Sep 24]. Available from: https://www.oxfordhandbooks.com/view/10.1093/oxfordhb/9 780199547029.001.0001/oxfordhb-9780199547029

121. Lengnick-Hall CA, Lengnick-Hall ML. Strategic Human Resources Management: A Review of the Literature and a Proposed Typology. Acad Manage Rev. 1988;13(3):454–70.

122. McWilliams A, Siegel D. Corporate Social Responsibility: A Theory of the Firm Perspective. Acad Manage Rev. 2001;26(1):117–27.

123. McWilliams A, Siegel DS, Wright PM. Corporate Social Responsibility: Strategic Implications*. J Manag Stud. 2006;43(1):1–18.

124. Hendry C, Pettigrew A. The Practice of Strategic Human Resource Management. Pers Rev. 1986 May 1;15(5):3–8.

125. Haque F. Importance of Strategic Human Resource Management [Internet]. The Strategy Watch. 2017 [cited 2021 Oct 13]. Available from: https://www.thestrategywatch.com/importance-strategic-human-resource-management/

126. wikipedia. Strategic fit. In: Wikipedia [Internet]. 2021 [cited 2021 Oct 13]. Available from: https://en.wikipedia.org/w/index.php?title=Strategic_fit&oldid=1008464607

127. Grant RM. Contemporary Strategy Analysis: Concepts, Techniques, Applications with Cases Set. 6th edition. Wiley-Blackwell; 2007. 946 p.

128. Shimizu K, Hitt MA. Strategic Flexibility: Organizational Preparedness to Reverse Ineffective Strategic Decisions. Acad Manag Exec 1993-2005. 2004;18(4):44–59.

129. Cingöz A, Akdoğan AA. Strategic Flexibility, Environmental Dynamism, and Innovation Performance: An Empirical Study. Procedia - Soc Behav Sci. 2013 Nov 6;99:582–9.

130. Wright PM, Snell SA. Toward a Unifying Framework for Exploring Fit and Flexibility in Strategic Human Resource Management. Acad Manage Rev. 1998;23(4):756–72.

131. Delery JE, Doty DH. Modes of Theorizing in Strategic Human Resource Management: Tests of Universalistic, Contingency, and Configurational Performance Predictions. Acad Manage J. 1996;39(4):802–35.

132. Vulpen E van. 7 Human Resource Best Practices (A mini-guide to HRM) [Internet]. AIHR. 2018 [cited 2023 Apr 12]. Available from: https://www.aihr.com/blog/human-resource-best-practices/

133. Prakash S. CuteHR. 2023 [cited 2023 Apr 7]. Top 10 HR Best Practices to build Better Workplaces in 2022. Available from: https://www.cutehr.io/hr-best-practices/

134. Team EC. Top 10 HR Best Practices [Internet]. Empxtrack. 2008 [cited 2023 Apr 7]. Available from: https://empxtrack.com/blog/top-10-hr-best-practices/

135. Young L. Applying research in practice: An analysis of the practical application of academic human resource best practices. In 2015 [cited 2023 Apr 7]. Available from:

https://www.semanticscholar.org/paper/Applying-research-in-practice%3A-An-analysis-of-the-Young/db354fa7aa2af3afa56795d7183b4c4bab5681c8

136. Pfeffer J, Hatano T, Santalainen T. Producing Sustainable Competitive Advantage through the Effective Management of People [and Executive Commentary]. Acad Manag Exec 1993-2005. 2005;19(4):95–108.

137. Boxall P, Purcell J. Strategy and Human Resource Management: Third Edition. Macmillan International Higher Education; 2011. 408 p.

138. Baird L, Meshoulam I. Managing Two Fits of Strategic Human Resource Management. Acad Manage Rev. 1988;13(1):116–28.

139. Schuler RS, Jackson SE. Linking Competitive Strategies with Human Resource Management Practices. Acad Manag Exec 1987-1989. 1987;1(3):207–19.

140. Ichniowski C, Shaw K, Prennushi G. The Effects of Human Resource Management Practices on Productivity: A Study of Steel Finishing Lines. Am Econ Rev. 1997;87(3):291–313.

141. ChatGPT. https://chat.openai.com/chat. 2023 [cited 2023 Apr 9]. Available from: https://chat.openai.com

.